ETHICS AND HUMAN RELATIONSHIPS

ETHICS AND HUMAN RELATIONSHIPS

by

Norman D. Hirsh

Carlton Press, Inc.   *New York, N.Y.*

To Peggy
My wife and friend

The author acknowledges permission to use quotes from *Situation Ethics* by Joseph Fletcher. Copyright ©MCMLXVI, W. L. Jenkins. Used by permission of The Westminster Press, and quotes from *The Ten Commandments* by Armin L. Robinson, copyright renewed ©1970 by Armin L. Robinson. Reprinted by permission of Simon & Schuster, Inc.

CONTENTS

PREFACE

Two reasons impelled me to write this book. I am dismayed at the waning of the moral impulse in American society. Ethics is increasingly seen as a luxury, not a necessity. Therefore, I have tried to clarify the moral foundations on which any lasting personal and group relationship must rest.

A second motivation compelled the writing of this book. I am a member of the present generation of a 3,800 year old people which, from its beginning, embarked on a journey of ethical discovery. From Abraham to Moses to Amos, from Hillel to the medieval writers of ethical wills to the Israeli authors of *The Seventh Day*, the Jew has searched passionately for what is good and right. I feel myself part of that 3,800 year old voyage of ethical discovery—a journey which fortunately has not yet ended. A voyage of discovery is always difficult, but I do not regret the difficulty, for I was not free to avoid the exploration. A force from the past, my inner being, the God of my fathers held me in an iron grip and would not release me until my part of the great journey was completed.

This book is not the creation of its author alone. My debts to others are profound.

I mention first my teachers. Richard Sewall of Yale University, who introduced me to the realism and nobility of tragic literature and its vision of life. Sheldon Blank of the Hebrew Union College-Jewish Institute of Religion, who shared his understanding of the ethical passion and perspective of the prophets of Israel and communicated to me a care for truth and a love of scholarship which he exemplifies in his own life.

I owe a special debt of gratitude to two friends who guided my studies in their fields of expertise. To J.G. Dash of the University of Washington, for directing my readings in the area of physics. And to James Mish'alani of the University of

Washington, who was my guide and teacher in the study of philosophy. Errors in my interpretation of physics and philosophy are my responsibility, not theirs.

Many friends helped me during the writing of this book. I am especially grateful to John Patrick Burke and Jane Schwartz for their encouragement and assistance.

I am thankful to the members of my congregation, Temple Beth Am of Seattle, Washington, who understood the scholarly needs of a rabbi and provided me with encouragement and ample vacation time for research and writing. They are to be commended for their commitment to Jewish scholarship.

To my parents, Esther and Milton Hirsh, peace unto them, I owe an incalculable debt.

A few remarks may be helpful to the reader of this volume. Chapter I serves as an introduction to the work; serious in its content, but more popular in tone than the succeeding chapters. Chapters II and III provide much of the groundwork for my discussion of the Ten Commandments in Chapter IV. Chapter V analyzes the golden rule and probes for the essence of the moral law. Chapter VI explores the territory of a newly discovered ethical law—the freedom rule. I encourage the reader to consult the notes to each chapter. I urge him to consider Note 19 to Chapter V.

The writing of this book required eight years. I commend it to the reader with the assurance that it is the product of a careful search to uncover the moral foundations which make for lasting personal relationships and for the survival of civilization itself. Completed with gratitude to the God of my fathers on this third day of July, 1975.

Norman D. Hirsh
Seattle, Washington

ETHICS AND HUMAN RELATIONSHIPS

Chapter I
WHY BE ETHICAL?

Why should we be ethical? Why should we keep a promise? Why should we tell the truth?

Ethical behavior has three purposes. These can be described as the immediate, the fundamental, and the motivating. I shall briefly discuss the most obvious purpose—the immediate, and then proceed to a more elaborate explanation of the fundamental and motivating purposes.

The Immediate Purpose

Helping the other human being is the immediate purpose of ethics. It is feeding the hungry, clothing the naked, healing the sick, granting rest to the weary, comforting the grief stricken, and providing opportunity for the oppressed. It is meeting the needs and securing the rights of the fellow human being.

The Fundamental Purpose

The fundamental purpose of ethics is constructive human relationships.[1] But what are constructive human relationships? Those relationships are constructive in which trust prevails, not distrust; in which honesty prevails, not lies, in which responsibility prevails, not indifference; in which respect prevails, not disrespect; in which love prevails, not hate.

In constructive human relationships, all persons are treated as equals in value; each is perceived not only as a means for

11

the fulfillment of others, but also as an end in himself;[2] and from such interactions of respect, a bond of caring grows.

In these relationships, people feel free to express their genuine feelings: there is true listening and speaking. Persons find the common human ground but respect their differences, and each supports the growth of the other as a human being capable of work and love,[3] faith and humor.[4] These relationships will endure.

We can better understand this ethical purpose if we invert the last five of the Ten Commandments. We would then be commanded:

> Thou shalt murder.
> Thou shalt commit adultery.
> Thou shalt steal.
> Thou shalt bear false witness.
> Thou shalt covet.

In a society based on these unethical commandments, constructive human relationships would be impossible. Trust would disintegrate; everyone becomes an enemy. Likewise, a society which repudiates the golden rule will soon fragment into hostile individuals and bitterly opposed groups. Ethical behavior is essential to the unity of a group. Therefore, it is even necessary that there be, as the saying goes, honor among thieves.

At this point, a question should be asked: Are not ethical behavior and constructive human relationships, as I have defined them, identical? They are not. Constructive human relationships involve dimensions which ethics cannot compel. Ethics alone will not make strangers into friends and friends into lovers. Social, cultural, psychological, and sexual factors influence the intensity of interaction. Ethics can only guarantee a necessary, but minimum, level of cooperation. Without ethics, however, the most intense relationship will disintegrate.

More intense constructive relationships require higher levels of ethical virtue than do less intense interactions. The honesty I can and should share with my wife, I am not required to share with a stranger. Constructive relationships, therefore, introduce new dimensions into ethics itself.

Ethics is essential to, but not the whole of, constructive human relationships. They are by no means identical. Therefore, we can properly understand constructive relationships as one of the goals of ethical behavior.

There is an apparent contradiction here. Ethical behavior does not always produce respect and trust between persons. This inconsistency can be easily explained. There must be a sufficient cause to produce the effect. If both parties fail in ethical endeavor, or if one party refuses to make a sufficient moral effort, the ethical force may be insufficient to produce a constructive relationship. But whenever the ethical input is sufficient, the invariable result is constructive relationship.

When there is injustice and groups are in conflict, the effect of ethical behavior on constructive relationships becomes complex. Let us take the example of a person who comes to the aid of oppressed migrant workers by opposing the actions of unjust growers. Once he acts, what happens? If his action is taken in a sensitive way, he will establish a constructive relationship with the migrant workers. Since the exploited feel especially alienated, this relationship is important. Even if their cause fails, his action has been of value because he established a human connection where it was both lacking and desperately needed. He has built a bridge to isolated human beings. In regard to the farm growers, his ethical action will lead to struggle and opposition in the short run. However, if he conducts his side of the conflict honestly, if he takes seriously the problems the growers face, if he remembers that the growers are human beings as well as opponents, he may in the long run establish a constructive relationship with them. The effect of his action on the basic conflict between the migrant workers and the farm owners must also be considered. In this regard, his action on behalf of justice offers the only hope of reconciling the antagonism between the migrants and the growers. For as long as the growers fail to treat the farm workers as human beings of equal value, no truly constructive relationships can develop between them. Thus, ethical action helps to set in motion forces which can lead to more constructive relationships.

The biblical prophets are a special and interesting case. They spoke truths so incredible and threatening to their contemporaries that it would be difficult to call the resulting relationships constructive. Perhaps they did establish constructive relationships with some of the poor and oppressed. However, the evidence we have indicates that most of their people were unwilling to accept criticism and critic. The ethical input came from one side only—the prophetic. Nevertheless, in the long run, the prophets made an immense contribution to constructive human relationships through their ethical teachings which shaped Jewish life and influenced western civilization.

The true cause and effect pattern is that ethical behavior causes constructive human relationships. Thus, ethics are as deeply rooted as natural law. When we understand its character, we realize that a moral order exists just as surely as a natural order. But the moral order does not connect ethics to success, it connects ethics to constructive relationships.

One of the greatest of the biblical prophets expressed the similarity of the moral to the natural order in a famous passage. The prophet Amos said:

> Do horses run up the cliff?
> Does one plow there with oxen?
> That you have turned justice into gall.
> And the fruit of righteousness into worm wood.[5]

Amos taught that it is as dangerous to pervert justice as it is to disregard the laws of nature. Justice is not merely a human ideal. It is rooted in the structure of life. Just as there are consequences to breaking physical laws, so there are consequences to breaking moral laws.

A similar analogy is drawn by E. M. Forster at the conclusion of his novel *A Passage to India*. Forster's novel takes place at the time when Britain rules India. The inequality in status between the Moslem, Aziz, the ruled, and his British friend, Fielding, the ruler, inevitably destroys their friendship. When ethics are violated, friendship cannot endure.[6] In the next to the last paragraph of the book, Fielding says to Aziz: "Why can't we be friends now? It's what I want. It's what you want."[7] Nevertheless, the final passage in the book describes their separation as if it were a physical necessity - their horses swerve apart, rocks divide them, the earth and the sky decree they cannot be friends.

The moral order is often undetected because we look for it in the wrong place. We shall not find a cause and effect pattern between ethics and success, but we will find a causal connection between ethics and constructive relationships. Before I analyze what the relationship is between ethics and success, I must briefly describe another direct consequence of ethical endeavor. Ethical action leads to the growth of character. An ethical person will not take advantage of others. He will thus develop habits of self examination, understanding of others, and self reliance. Because he is committed to doing the right even at the cost of material gain and popularity, he will free himself from slavery to material goods and public approval. He thus becomes a person of character, free to make hard, necessary and moral decisions. Such a person realizes that nothing is more important than preserving his moral self. The commitment to preserve a moral self is the motivating purpose of the ethical life. Of this, more later.

The purpose of ethics is not success in business or victory in battle. In so far as the advantages of character and constructive relationships influence the outcome of events, ethics will be influential. A good example is the democratic leadership practiced by the officers in Israel's army. The willingness of these officers to discuss tactics with their men before the battle, and to lead rather than follow in the attack, contributes to victory. On the other hand, evil does tend to destroy itself. During the Second World War, Hermann Göring, arrogant Commander-in-Chief of the Luft-waffe refused to believe that the English could have achieved a more highly efficient radar system than German science had developed. Göring's arrogance led to a decisive error in judgment.[8] Nevertheless, although ethical behavior usually produces favorable results and unethical behavior negative results, there are no guarantees. One of the best kings in Jewish history, Josiah, was killed in 608 B.C.E.[9] at Megiddo when the Judean army was overwhelmed by a superior Egyptian force. In our own time, six million Jews died for no ethical fault of their own.

Ethics contributes to survival, success, and happiness through the agency of constructive relationships and character. These qualities are the best hope for the survival of the group because groups usually perish from inner divisions and character disintegration. It is worth noting that two civilizations, the Jewish and Chinese, built on ethical foundations have survived the vicissitudes of history. Nevertheless, basically decent civilizations such as certain American Indian tribes have been swept away by adverse historical circumstances.

A life of integrity and constructive relationships will almost always bring inner happiness. The ethical person will experience as the deepest satisfactions life can offer, the joy of virtue and the wonder of enduring relationship. Nevertheless, we may well conceive of a person who has paid a terrible price, including the suffering of his loved ones, for the sake of a good cause, questioning the value of his sacrifice. Such a person experiences agony as well as satisfaction of spirit. Not every modern person can summon up the moral enthusiasm of the ancient moralists who felt that no torture or torment could diminish the inner joy virtue brings.

Ethics contributes to, but is not a sufficient cause for, survival, success, and even happiness. There is no direct and inevitable cause and effect pattern here. Overwhelming forces like disease, war, poverty, and historical change may intervene to engulf the ethical individual or nation. There is a powerful tragic dimension to life. In some situations, no amount of ethical endeavor is sufficient to achieve safety, victory, or even contentment of spirit. We should neither discount nor exaggerate the contribution of ethics to outer success and inner happiness. The contribution is very considerable, but not always decisive. The longer the time span involved, the greater the probability that goodness will be vindicated, and evil prove self destructive. The larger the group involved, the greater the probability that the good community will outlast its misfortunes and that the evil community will precipitate its own demise. When we approach the scale of humankind and its long-term future, ethical action is the only hope for survival. This is true because humanity's only dangerous enemy is itself. If we can cooperate with each other and respect our environment, we can survive. But, if humankind as a whole continues to waste precious resources on war, accepts the accelerating division between rich and poor, fails to build true communities, and abuses the environment, then we may be quite sure that we have no future. A bold image from the Talmud[10] applies to the human situation. When Israel stood at Mount Sinai, the Talmud says that God held the mountain over the head of the people and declared: "If you accept the Torah, well and good; if not, this will be your grave."[11]

Ethics is the best hope for survival, success, and especially happiness. Nevertheless, it is clear that these goals may sometimes be incompatible with ethics. In unusual circumstances, for example, an ethical person may have to sacrifice his life rather than betray his principles. In the fourth century C.E., a rabbinic sage, Raba, advised a man who was commanded by the mayor of his town to kill another man or else be killed himself, to suffer death rather than commit murder. Raba told the man that he could not assume that his life was more valuable than the other man's.[12] The purpose of ethics is not survival, success or happiness.

We can make a rough diagram of the overall pattern:

```
                        constructive
                        human
                        relationships   contributes to
              causes    (fundamental
                        purpose)

ethics    helping                                       survival
          persons                                       success
          (immediate                                    happiness
          purpose)   causes        contributes to

                        character
                        (motivating
                        purpose)
```

There is a cause and effect relationship between ethics and constructive human relationships and growth of character. There is not a cause and effect pattern between ethics and survival, success, or even happiness. Ethics is, however, more closely connected to happiness than it is to survival or success.

The Motivating Purpose

Even though constructive relationships are the fundamental purpose of ethics, they are not the motivating purpose. An examination of a difficult ethical situation reveals the motivating purpose in ethical decision making. Rabbi Jacob Soetendorp, a liberal rabbi in Amsterdam, told me the following true story. During the Second World War, the Nazis interrogated a Christian who had arranged for the concealment of many Jewish families. This man's wife was pregnant at that time. The Nazis said to him: "We will kill you before the eyes of your wife unless you tell us where five Jewish families are hiding." Then they brought in his wife. He said to her: "I cannot tell, forgive me, my wife." She replied: "You must do what is right. I will endure it." The Nazis killed him in her presence. Why did this man refuse to reveal the hiding places of the Jews? Why did he sacrifice his life?

We may rule out as the primary motivation the fundamental purpose of ethics—constructive human relationships. In the first place, no one worries about the effect of his decision on the quality of human relationships in such a searing moment of crisis. In the second place, even such real ties of compassion as he may have with the projected victims, will prove insufficient weighed against the will to survive. He may visualize the hidden Jewish families in his mind, but the threat of death will overwhelm compassion. John Stuart Mill believed that "the social feelings of mankind" could serve as the firm foundation of morality.[13] I do not disparage this motivation. It can be strong. Yet, pitted against the will to survive or even the will to succeed compassion will not prove decisive. People are adept at limiting their involvement. When we get past the immediate family, all kinds of rationalizations come into play. The human bond is just not that strong.

18

Why did the good man of our example refuse to betray the hidden Jews? He did what he did becuse it was right, simply because it was right. But why, we may ask, was he so committed to doing what was right?

In the moment of decision, we do the right because we cannot betray our moral selves. It is *self* preservation on the noblest level. We say of the unethical act which tempts us: I just can't do it. It's not right. Or if confronted by the need for positive action, we say: I must do it. It's the right thing to do. If we pursue these qustions asking ourselves why we are so attached to doing the right, we will finally answer: I am a human being. A human being cares about right and wrong. Or we may reply: I am a Jew. A Jew cares about right and wrong. Or we may say: I am a Christian. A Christian cares about right and wrong. Whatever answer we give, we affirm a moral identity.

I believe that the good man of our example gave up his life rather than surrender his moral self. He chose to die loyal to his moral self, rather than betray what gives a human being nobility and worth. We are not honest, for example, because honesty is the best policy. We are honest at bedrock because we abhor dishonesty and cannot accept it in ourselves. No one ever expressed the deepest reason for morality better than the ancient hero Job, who, despite rejection by his friends and argument with God, refused to betray the truth as he had come to know it, saying: "Till I die I will not put away my integrity from me."[14]

If we examine great moral decisions, again and again we will discover that a moral self concept is the most powerful mechanism for the ethical life. In December, 1955, during the Montgomery bus boycott, a Black minister working for the car pool system picked up a woman walking. He said, "Sister, aren't you getting tired?" She replied, "My soul has been tired for a long time. Now my feet are tired, and my soul is resting."[15]

A moral self concept is crucial. Mogens Fisker, a Dane who helped many Jews to escape from the Nazis in World War II, described the rescue as "simply the human thing to do."[16] And Aubrey Hodes, a young Israeli disciple of Martin Buber, in describing how he saved a wounded Arab civilian from death at the hands of some Israeli soldiers during the Six Day War wrote, "If I had failed him, I would have failed myself."[1][7]

Compassion helps move us to do the right. But for the most difficult ethical decisions, we must rely on a deeper motivation. We must count on our unwillingness to betray our moral selves. In the moment of decision, if we are fortunate, we cannot betray what most makes us human. Thus, even in a losing cause, human beings can do the right and preserve a moral self.

Even in a losing cause, an ethical human being can achieve two noble purposes. He can build a bridge to others who are oppressed. And he can preserve his moral self. Thus, in 1943, in the Warsaw Ghetto, doomed Jews wrote their journals and died resisting the Nazi evil. They wanted their story known. They died refusing to submit passively to evil.

Whoever builds bridges to the oppressed and preserves his moral self has achieved two of the three great purposes of ethics. He may fail to liberate the oppressed, but he has not totally failed. On the other hand, the person who acts unethically has not helped his fellow human being, has not built the human connections and has not preserved his moral self. He has truly failed.

The sage Hillel was the spiritual leader of the Jewish people from 30 B.C.E. to 10 C.E. One of his most famous sayings emphasizes the importance of a moral self concept. Hillel's maxim also recognizes the complexity of life and gives classic expression to the Jewish view that we have duties both to ourselves and to others. Hillel's saying divides into three parts:

> If I am not for myself, who will be for me?
> And if I am only for myself, what am I?
> And if not now, when?[1][8]

The first part of the saying acknowledges that life is often a jungle: that if I do not defend myself, no one else will. The third part teaches that the time for moral action is now, not some other more propitious occasion. It is the second part of the maxim which speaks to the issue of moral identity. If I defend only myself and thus deny the bond to the other human being, what am I? Have I not reduced myself to a jungle animal struggling to survive? If I reject the relationships and responsibilities which make human, how can I claim a human identity? In just two Hebrew words, אני מה , what am I, Hillel penetrated to the heart of moral identity and illumined the deepest source of ethical motivation.[19]

The situation of humankind is desperate enough as it is. It would be far more desperate if ethics had to rely for motivation on a mechanism less powerful than the moral self concept. Of course, if societies fail to develop a moral self concept, then the mechanism for ethics fails. A moral identity is not automatic; it must be developed by the family and society. The Talmud clearly taught this crucial truth when it declared that the evil inclination, the *yazer hara*, enters the individual at birth, but the good inclination, the *yazer tov*, is not manifest until thirteen.[20] The good inclination thus requires nurturing. Aristotle expressed the same idea differently. He said that in order to understand what is noble and just a person "must have been brought up in good habits."[21]

Why be ethical? The simple and direct answer is to help people. But the immediate purpose, valid as it is, does not penetrate to the deepest reasons for the ethical life. Ethics has a purpose deeper than itself.

Without ethics, there cannot be constructive human relationships. These relationships are the fundamental purpose of ethics. They are also for the secular person the purpose of life, and for the religious person a straight road to the purpose of life. We serve God by loving humanity.[22] We often wish that ethics would invariably lead to survival, success, and happiness. It doesn't. But ethics does lead, according to our different beliefs, to life's human or divine purpose. Loving and enduring human relationships are the fundamental purpose of ethics.

Nevertheless, if you ask yourself in the moment of decision, "Why should I be ethical?" asking in all the passion and uncertainty of life, then you may find the answer by asking Hillel's question—"What am I?" Phrase it in the modern idiom—what kind of a person am I? We are moral beings. We are ethical to preserve a moral self. To keep alive

21

in the midst of life's corruption that quality which gives human existence nobility and worth. This is the deepest motivating purpose of the ethical life. The moral self concept is the mechanism of ethics.

Ethical behavior has three purposes. Helping persons is the immediate purpose. Constructive human relationships is the fundamental purpose. Preserving a moral self is the motivating purpose. We need purposes beyond the self. We need a motivation as close as the self.

NOTES

1. I am indebted to the late Abraham Cronbach, Professor of Social Studies at the Hebrew-Union College, for the phrase: "constructive human relationships." I recall Professor Cronbach saying that the purpose of *religion* is constructive human relationships.

2. Immanuel Kant, *Foundations of the Metaphysics of Morals.* Indianapolis and New York: Bobbs-Merrill, 1959, p.47.

3. Erik H. Erikson, *Childhood and Society.* New York: W. W. Norton and Company, 1950, p. 229. In his old age, Freud was once asked what a normal person should be able to do well. Freud is reported to have answered, *"Lieben und arbeiten,"* to love and to work.

4. Aubrey Hodes, *Martin Buber—An Intimate Portrait.* New York: Viking Press, 1971, p. 134. Buber commented on Freud's answer, saying it was not complete. He (Buber) would say, "Work, love, faith, and humor." By faith in this context, I mean primarily faith in life and its possibilities.

5. Amos 6:12. There is some possibility the second verse should be translated, "Does one plow the sea with oxen?"

6. Ethics consists of mercy as well as justice. Considerable disparities in status may, on some occasions, be overcome if mercy is powerful enough to forgive and accept. Yet, to violate justice is to threaten the relationship. Inequalities in status as severe as Forster describes, if perpetuated, almost inevitably shatter a relationship.

7. E. M. Forster, *A Passage to India.* New York: Harcourt, Brace and World, Inc., A Harvest Book, 1924, p. 322.

8. Derek Wood and Derek Dempster, *The Narrow Margin.* New York, Toronto, London: McGraw-Hill Book Company, 1961, p. 26.

9. Throughout this book, I use the traditional Jewish abbreviations: B.C.E., Before the Common Era, and C.E., The Common Era. The dates are the same as the Christian B.C. and A.D., but a Jew cannot use expressions like "Before Christ," and "Anno Domini."

10. The Talmud is a vast collection of Jewish law and wisdom completed in the Fifth Century C.E. There are a Palestinian and a

Babylonian Talmud. The Babylonian Talmud is more complete and important.

11. The Babylonian Talmud, Shabbat 88a.

12. The Babylonian Talmud, Pesahim 25b.
13. Smith and Sosa, *Mill's Utilitarianism*. Belmont, California: Wadsworth, 1969, p. 58.

14. Job 27:5.

15. *Time Magazine*, January 16, 1956, p. 20.

16. Harold Flender, *Rescue in Denmark*. New York: MacFadden Books, 1964, p. 14.

17. Aubrey Hodes, *Martin Buber—An Intimate Portrait*. New York: Viking Press, 1971, p. 40.

18. Joseph H. Hertz, *Sayings of the Fathers*. New York: Behrman House, Inc., 1945, p. 25.

19. There are varying interpretations of Hillel's saying. See, for example, R. Travers Herford, *The Ethics of the Talmud: Sayings of the Fathers*, New York, Schocken Books, 1962, p. 34. While nobody knows exactly what Hillel intended, I believe my interpretation is faithful to the plain sense of the maxim, explains the tension between parts one and two (which other explanations conspicuously fail to do) and is in accord with Hillel's personality as a man passionately concerned with ethics. Hillel was the formulator of the golden rule for the western world.

20. A. Cohen, *Everyman's Talmud*. London: J. M. Dent and Sons, Ltd., 1949, p. 89.

21. Richard McKeon, *Introduction to Aristotle*. New York: Random House, Inc., The Modern Library, 1947, pp. 311, 312.

22. For the religious person, the ultimate purpose of life is to serve God. But how do we serve God? Through building the human connections. The major thrust of Jewish teaching is that a person loves God by loving his fellow human beings. Through human relationships, not apart from them, we approach God.
In Jewish theology, the human being is a "co-worker with God" in

24

the ongoing process of creation. For the specific phrase, see Babylonian Talmud, Shabbat 119b. If the human connections develop, a messianic age can be achieved. The hope for the messianic age is the indestructible hope of Judaism. And every hope, especially this one, must become a duty.

The Jewish philosopher, Hermann Cohen, described humankind's duty as the creation of a united humanity. Cohen explained that in nature, man is only *beside* the other man (*Nebenmensch*). Their relations are antagonistic. But through an ethical relationship, man lives not only side by side, but *with* another (*Mitmensch*). Man's duty is to transform himself from natural man (*Nebenmensch*) into fellow-man (*Mitmensch*). See Samuel Hugo Bergman, *Faith and Reason: An Introduction to Modern Jewish Thought*, New York: Schocken Books, 1963, p. 51.

Chapter II
WHAT IS A MORAL LAW?

Moral laws are essential to the ethical life. They express the ethical interactions necessary to constructive human relationships.

We life in a universe of law. Our world is a cosmos, an orderly system, not a chaos. And the human mind is well attuned to discover the laws of the universe.

The discovery of the neutrino serves as a brilliant example of the lawfulness of the universe. In 1934, Enrico Fermi predicted the existence of the neutrino. In certain kinds of radioactive decay, not enough energy was being emitted from the nucleus of the atom to preserve one of the most basic principles of physics—the principle of the conservation of mass-energy. Another basic principle, that of conservation of momentum, was also threatened. There seemed to be no explanation for this disturbing fact. Fermi postulated that an as yet unknown particle with no charge and very little mass, but with the "missing" energy was escaping from the nucleus. Fermi called this unknown particle the neutrino. For over twenty years, all attempts to find a neutrino failed. But so deeply embedded is the principle of the conservation of mass-energy that physicists did not abandon the neutrino hypothesis. It simply had to exist. In 1956, superb experiments located the neutrino. Fermi was right. Only in a spectacularly lawful universe could the neutrino have been predicted and discovered.

There are many kinds of law. A good way to understand moral law is to compare it to scientific law.

Similarities Between Scientific and Moral Laws

What does a scientific law do? A scientific law expresses the relationship between different aspects of a physical phenomenon.[1] Thus, Einstein revealed the connections between energy and matter in the formula $E = mc^2$ (energy equals mass times the speed of light squared). Ohm's Law provides us with another example. Ohm revealed the relationship of the electromotive force, voltage, to the strength of the electric current actually flowing, amperage, in the formula $V = I \times R$ (voltage equals amperes times the resistance). Heisenberg's Uncertainty Principle focuses on the relationship of the uncertainties of momentum and position in the atomic realm. His formula states that the uncertainty in momentum times the uncertainty in position is equal to or greater than a number which physicists refer to as "Planck's constant." Thus it is impossible to simultaneously measure with precision the momentum and position of a small particle such as an electron. These examples indicate that a scientific law expresses the relationship between aspects of a physical phenomenon. These relationships or connections exhibit a regularity which makes law possible.

A moral law is similar. A moral law expresses the ethical interactions necessary to constructive relationships between persons. The golden rule reveals what is essential in order to connect person to person harmoniously: "What is hateful to you, do not do to your neighbor." Likewise, it is clear that the injunction: "Keep your promises," is a rule which defines one aspect of constructive relationship between persons. Friendships can hardly be based on broken promises. Kant's categorical imperative provides an excellent example of what a moral law does. The categorical imperative states: "Act only according to that maxim by which you can at the same time will that it should be a universal law." The individual is thus warned against making an exception of himself and setting himself above those standards of morality which distinguish a humane society from a jungle. If the categorical imperative is flouted, human relationships in society soon move in the direction of what Thomas Hobbes called the war of "every man against every man."[2]

Both scientific and moral laws express the nature of the connections which regulate the real world. Scientific laws illuminate the physical connections. Moral laws illuminate basic dimensions of the personal connections.

Differences Between Scientific and Moral Laws

Scientific and moral laws are similar. Nevertheless, there

are several significant differences which should not be overlooked between these two types of laws. One difference immediately emerges. The form of expression is different. Scientific laws are usually formulated in mathematical terms. Ethical laws are not. Mathematics is the tool of science. Language is the tool of ethics.

Another distinction between these two types of laws is readily apparent. Ethics must take into account the free choice of persons. That is why a moral law cannot simply state the relationship between persons; it must express what is, given the nature of human beings, *constructive* relationship. Scientific laws dealing with physical phenomena simply describe what the relationship is. No questions of freedom are involved.

Another difference emerges from the reality of freedom. Since human beings are free, ethical laws take the form of imperatives. They convey the sense of ought so that in the difficult arena of choice, persons will choose as well as know the right.

Another difference relates to the method of verification. A scientific law is established by the scientific method. Integral to this method is the making of observations, the discovery of patterns, the formulation of a hypothesis, testing to confirm or refute the hypothesis, and, if confirmed, further testing to determine the scope of the newly discovered law. There are no comparable means to validate a moral law. A moral law is established by conscience and experience. We are dealing with two different areas of truth, and the means of responsibly accepting these truths differ. Once acquired, we even hold these truths in different ways. It is not absurd to say that I once knew Ohm's Law, but now I have forgotten it. It is, however, absurd to say that I once knew the difference between right and wrong, but now I have forgotten it.[3]

Science and Ethics Solidly Grounded

There are real differences between scientific and moral laws because they operate in different realms. But the fact of a significant similarity remains. Both kinds of laws illuminate the connections which exist in the real world. A scientific law expresses the relationship between aspects of a physical phenomenon. A moral law expresses the moral interactions basic to constructive relationship between persons. Just as science is grounded in the nature of physical interactions, so ethics is grounded in the nature of human interactions.

Our knowledge of ethical law is more solidly grounded than our knowledge of scientific law. Newton's laws of motion were modified by Einstein's discoveries.[4] The Ten Commandments have not been qualified by the discoveries of subsequent moral philosophers. The sociological dimensions of the Ten Commandments have changed; the ethical imperatives, however, remain constant and valid.

We may, therefore, have more confidence in our ethical understanding than in our scientific understanding. The primary reason for this disparity is that the tools appropriate to ethical investigation are less sophisticated than the tools necessary for scientific measurement. The observations and insights necessary to ethical discovery were as readily available to Moses as they were to Kant. The same cannot be said if we compare the scientific work of Aristotle and Einstein.

Moral laws exist apart from man's knowledge of them. The ethical interactions at the heart of constructive human relationships, discovered or undiscovered, are a reality just as surely as the interactions of energy and matter were a reality before and after Einstein. Of course, an individual formulates the law. He may even use an invented tool like language or mathematics in his formulation. But the source of the law is not the fertile invention of the human mind. The source of the law is the complex structure of God's creation. Moral laws are discovered, not invented. Moses discovered the Ten Commandments; he did not invent them.

The Centrality of Moral Law

The moral law is central to the ethical life. It is more than the preference of an individual or a society. The moral law is firmly rooted in the ongoing nature of human relationship itself. Thus, it is established in a commanding position outside the individual.

There are some who believe that moral laws stand in the way of the ethical life. They claim that only good will

30

combined with sensitivity to the complexity of situations can lead to truly good behavior. Others, despairing of traditional values in a changing age, call upon the individual to listen to "the ten thousand commandments implied in the ten thousand situations of which his life consists."[5]

These advisors are misguided. They do not understand the authority and the complexity of the moral law. They propose a false choice between obedience to the moral law and sensitivity to the situation. Many things are important for the moral life. A sensitivity to the complexity of situations is one. A deep feeling that persons are precious is another. A recognition of how unethical behavior leads to the fragmentation and insecurity of life is still another. Absolutely essential is a firm commitment to preserve a moral self. Allied to this commitment is the acceptance of the moral law. For the moral law both tells us what is right and commands us to do it. In the trials of life, it sums up our duty into a profound moral idea which clarifies and persuades. A moral self will understand and hold to the moral law as the supreme expression of ethical requirement.

In the tests of life, good will fails us. The difficulties of the human situation provoke our hatred, our jealousy, our lust. It is only the moral law and our capacity to respond to it, which returns us to our duty.

Rabbi Leo Baeck was one of a few hundred survivors of 45,000 Jews at Theresienstadt concentration camp. When the Russians liberated the camp, they turned over some camp officials to the survivors for slaughter. But Leo Baeck stood up and pleaded for the lives of the officials. Despite what they had done, he argued that they still remained the wards of justice and, as such, deserved a fair trial.

What enabled Leo Baeck to defend the rights of even the concentration camp officials? It was not good will. Nor was there anything in the situation that could adequately stir Baeck to decency. Rather, in the crisis, Baeck managed to hear the old commandments: "Thou shalt not take vengeance." "Thou shalt not murder." Ethical action requires a moral self capable of hearing the moral law.

An ethical person seeks to live by the moral law. The trials and tests of life can easily dehumanize us. But the moral law recalls us to our moral selves and re-establishes the human bond.

31

NOTES

1. See Carl G. Hempel, *Philosophy of Natural Science*, Englewood Cliffs, New Jersey; Prentice Hall, 1966, p. 54.

2. Thomas Hobbes, *Leviathan*, Baltimore, Maryland: Penguin Books, 1968, p. 185.

3. See Gilbert Kyle, "On Forgetting the Difference Between Right and Wrong," in A. I. Melden, ed., *Essays in Moral Philosophy*, Seattle and London: University of Washington, 1958, p. 147ff.

4. Thomas S. Kuhn, *The Structure of Scientific Revolutions*, Chicago, Illinois: The University of Chicago Press, 1970, pp. 101, 102. Also Leopold Infeld, *Albert Einstein*, New York, New York: Charles Scribner's Sons, 1950, p. 26.

5. Viktor E. Frankl, *The Will to Meaning*, New York and Cleveland: The World Publishing Company, 1969, p. X.

Chapter III
MORAL PRINCIPLES AND MORAL RULES

There are two kinds of moral laws: moral principles and moral rules. The differences between them make it possible for the moral law to be both flexible enough for complicated situations and firm enough for universal applications.

How can we distinguish between moral principles and moral rules? Let us test a moral law such as the seventh commandment—"Thou shalt not commit adultery"—against a situation from the Second World War. This case is described by Joseph Fletcher in his book, *Situation Ethics:*

As the Russian armies drove westward to meet the Americans and British at the Elbe, a Soviet patrol picked up a Mrs. Bergmeier foraging food for her three children. Unable even to get word to the children, and without any clear reason for it, she was taken off to a prison camp in the Ukraine. Her husband had been captured in the Bulge and taken to a POW camp in Wales.

When he was returned to Berlin, he spent weeks and weeks rounding up his children; two (Ilse, twelve, and Paul, ten) were found in a detention school run by the Russians, and the oldest, Hans, fifteen, was found hiding in a cellar near the Alexander Platz. Their mother's whereabouts remained a mystery, but they never stopped searching. She more than anything else was needed to reknit them as a family in that dire situation of hunger, chaos, and fear.

Meanwhile, in the Ukraine, Mrs. Bergmeier learned through a sympathetic commandant that her husband and family were trying to keep together and find her. But the rules allowed them to release her for only two reasons: (1) illness needing medical facilities beyond the camp's, in which case she would be sent to a Soviet hosptial elsewhere, and (2) pregnancy, in which case she would be returned to Germany as a liability.

She turned things over in her mind and finally asked a friendly Volga German camp guard to impregnate her,

33

which he did. Her condition being medically verified, she was sent back to Berlin and to her family. They welcomed her with open arms, even when she told them how she had managed it. When the child was born, they loved him more than all the rest, on the view that little Dietrich had done more for them than anybody.

When it was time for him to be christened, they took him to the pastor on a Sunday afternoon. After the ceremony, they sent Dietrich home with the children and sat down in the pastor's study, to ask whether they were right to feel as they did about Mrs. Bergmeier and Dietrich. Should they be grateful to the Volga German? Had Mrs. Bergmeier done a good and right thing?[1]

Mrs. Bergmeier's intent was fidelity; nevertheless, she committed adultery. We cannot evade the conclusion, however, that Mrs. Bergmeier was right in setting aside the seventh commandment. This unusual case, therefore, constitutes a genuine exception to the seventh commandment.

Moral Rules

The seventh commandment is a moral rule. For moral rules, unlike moral principles, require exceptions. John Stuart Mill stated it most concisely:

It is not the fault of any creed, but of the complicated nature of human affairs, that rules of conduct cannot be so framed as to require no exceptions, and that hardly any kind of action can safely be laid down as either always obligatory or always condemnable.[2]

In his book, *Generalization in Ethics*, Marcus G. Singer clarifies the distinction between principles and rules. Rules, as we have seen, allow exceptions. They state what is usually right or wrong, but there are occasions when it is not only justified, but imperative to break a moral rule.[3] In some situations, a parent should steal milk for his starving child.

Moral principles, on the other hand, allow no exceptions. They are also deeper than and the source of moral rules. Thus, we often speak of the principle underlying a certain rule which determines its scope and justifies exceptions to it.[4] Moral principles are not only more fundamental than rules; they are also more general and comprehensive. It follows that principles are necessarily more abstract than rules.[5]

Given these conditions, it is clear that moral principles will not be nearly as numerous as moral rules. What are some moral principles?

Kant's categorical imperative is such a principle: "Act only according to that maxim by which you can at the same time will that it should become a universal law."[6] In other words, when faced with an ethical choice, we must ask the question, "What if everyone in a similar situation were to do that?" The categorical imperative, thus, warns the individual not to make an exception of himself and not to set himself above the moral law.

There are exceptional situations, but no person is an exception. The Torah, the five books of Moses, speaks strongly on this point. None is above the law. Not the powerful and not the king.[7] Even the poor, for whom the Torah has immense compassion, are not to be favored at the expense of justice.[8] This truth also implies that no people, no nation, and no religion is above the moral law.

A second moral principle is Mill's principle of utility: "Actions are right in proportion as they tend to promote happiness; wrong as they tend to produce the reverse of happiness."[9] This is sometimes called the greatest happiness principle. Mill did not intend by this principle to dispense with moral rules. But when moral rules conflict, when it becomes difficult to ascertain what is right, the principle of utility serves as a standard for decision.[10]

Another moral principle (whose special status will be discussed later) is Hillel's version of the golden rule: "What is hateful unto you, do not do unto thy neighbor."[11] When making a decision, a person should ask himself the question, "How would I like that done to me?" The golden rule places persons on the same level of value, and encourages one person to consider the feelings of another.

It is relatively easy to see how either the categorical imperative or the principle of utility or the golden rule could serve as the source or reason for a moral rule such as the prohibition of stealing.

There are other moral principles somewhat less comprehensive and less deep than these. They, too, will admit of no exceptions, but they are not relevant in every case. Singer mentions, as less comprehensive moral principles: it is always wrong to cause unnecessary suffering, killing for the sake of killing is always wrong, stealing for the sake of stealing is always wrong, lying for the sake of lying is always wrong, and so on.[12]

Moral Principles are Universal

There are decisive differences between moral principles and moral rules. The failure to distinguish between these two types of moral laws has caused considerable confusion in moral thought. Moral rules permit exceptions and may not be binding in every situation in our own or other societies. In a society where mutual suspicion and hostility prevail, where truth telling is dangerous in the extreme, the rule against lying may have to be set aside. But a moral principle is always and everywhere obligatory.[13] When the Indians of the Hudson Bay territory first obtained guns, they hunted Eskimos for sport. This practice continued until the Eskimos got guns. What can we say of this practice of the Hudson Bay Indian community? We can say it was wrong. It violates the golden rule, the categorical imperative, the principle of utility, and the principle that killing for the sake of killing is always wrong. There are universal moral laws!

Moral principles are universal. They are not the preferences of particular individuals or societies. They are rooted in the nature of the human relationship itself. It is, therefore, valuable to observe that a great principle like the golden rule has been independently discovered in many civilizations at different times.

The Discovery of the Golden Rule
in Different Civilizations

The Golden Rule first appears in Jewish literature in the first few centuries B.C.E. in the Book of Tobit and in the Testaments of the Twelve Patriarchs. But Hillel (leader of the Jewish people from 30 B.C.E. to 10 C.E.) gave it classical expression. A would-be convert came to Hillel and asked the sage to teach him the whole of the Torah while he, the prospective convert, stood on one foot. Hillel replied, "What is hateful unto you, do not do unto thy neighbor. That is the whole of the Torah. The rest is commentary. Go and learn."[14] Some years after Hillel, Jesus gave the golden rule a positive formualtion: "Whatever you wish that men would do to you, do so to them; for this is the law and the prophets."[15]

In the fifth century B.C.E., Confucius stated the golden rule in its negative form.[16] In that same century, Buddha taught the golden rule in both positive and negative forms. Plato, in the fourth century B.C.E., formulated the golden rule. The Stoics, Seneca and Epictetus, in the first century C.E. gave particularly powerful expression to this moral principle. Epictetus wrote, "What you avoid suffering, do not attempt to make others suffer. You avoid slavery; take care that others are not your slaves." The golden rule is eloquently stated in the ancient Hindu texts, the Upanishads, which date back to the 8th century B.C.E. Fifteen hundred years later in the Pahlavi texts of the Zoroastrian literature, the golden rule is also taught. But the golden rule has been discovered not only by the famous sages of mankind and inscribed in the well known sacred literature of the world. What we may call, perhaps wrongly, simpler peoples, have also seen its truth. An African tribe the Ba-Congo, teaches: "O man, what you do not like, do not to your fellows." And Moroccan tribesmen proclaim the golden rule in its positive form.

This survey of the independent discovery[17] of the golden rule in so many different civilizations should indicate that sweeping moral relativism is misguided. Some values are relative. But moral principles are universal. Wherever there are persons, moral principles obligate.

Moral Systems

Both principles and rules are necessary. To be adequate, every moral system must have a comprehensive moral principle and incisive moral rules. The moral principle is essential as the ground for universal standards, the source for rules, and the basis for decision in difficult cases. The moral rules are necessary to deter rationalization and to meet the specific issues of life. "Thou shalt not steal" has a direct and immediate power which the golden rule cannot match. In the next chapter, I will discuss a basic moral system, the Ten Commandments.

However complex and admirable a moral system may be, we should never for a moment overlook the fact that such a system is not self-operative. Human beings are the ones who sensitively analyze the situation and embrace the moral laws. This, I believe, is what Leo Baeck meant when he said that there is no justice without just human beings.

NOTES

1. Joseph Fletcher, *Situation Ethics*, Philadelphia: Westminister, 1966, pp. 164, 165.

2. Smith and Sosa, *Mill's Utilitarianism*, Belmont, California: Wadsworth, 1969, p. 53.

3. In A. I. Melden, ed., *Essays in Moral Philisophy*, Seattle and London: University of Washington, 1958, p. 165.

4. ibid p. 160

5. ibid p. 169.

6. Immanuel Kant, *Foundations of the Metaphysics of Morals*, Indianapolis and New York: Bobbs-Merrill, 1959, p. 39. Another formulation of the categorical imperative is: "Act so that you treat humanity, whether in your own person or in that of another, always as an end and never as a means only." Ibid p. 47. Kant, however, considered the formulation which focuses on "a universal law" to be the preferred expression of the categorical imperative. See ibid p. 55.

7. Leviticus 19:15, Deuteronomy 17:14-20.

8. Exodus 23:3, Leviticus 19:15.

9. Smith and Sosa, p. 36.

10. ibid pp. 52, 53.

11. Babylonian Talmud, Shabbat 31a.

12. A. I, Melden, p. 174.

13. ibid, p. 194ff.

14. Babylonian Talmud, Shabbat 31a.

15. Matthew 7:12.

16. The examples given in this paragraph are to be found in the *International Journal of Ethics*, Volume XLIV, July 1934, No. 4. "On Golden Rules," by J. O. Hertzler.

17. In the above survey, there may be a few examples of borrowing. But independent discovery is the overwhelming fact which emerges from this overview.

Chapter IV
THE TEN WORDS

The Ten Words from Exodus, Chapter 20, according to the Jewish numeration:

And God spoke all these words saying:
1. I am the Lord thy God, who brought thee out of the land of Egypt, out of the house of bondage.

2. Thou shalt have no other gods before Me. Thou shalt not make unto thee a graven image, nor any manner of likeness, of any thing that is in heaven above, or that is in the earth beneath, or that is in the water under the earth; thou shalt not bow down unto them, nor serve them; for I the Lord thy God am a jealous God, visiting the iniquity of the fathers upon the children unto the third and fourth generation of them that hate Me; and showing mercy unto the thousandth generation of them that love Me and keep My commandments.

3. Thou shalt not take the name of the Lord thy God in vain; for the Lord will not hold him guiltless that taketh His name in vain.

4. Remember the sabbath day, to keep it holy. Six days shalt thou labor, and do all thy work; but the seventh day is a sabbath unto the Lord thy God, in it thou shalt not do any manner of work, thou, nor thy son, nor thy daughter, nor thy man-servant, nor thy maid-servant, nor thy cattle, nor thy stranger that is within thy gates; for in six days the Lord made heaven and earth, the sea, and all that in them is, and rested on the seventh day; wherefore the Lord blessed the sabbath day and hallowed it.

5. Honour thy father and thy mother, that thy

days may be long upon the land which the Lord
thy God giveth thee.

6. Thou shalt not murder.

7. Thou shalt not commit adultery.

8. Thou shalt not steal.

9. Thou shalt not bear false witness against thy
neighbour.

10. Thou shalt not covet thy neighbour's house; thou
shalt not covet thy neighbour's wife, nor his
man-servant, nor his maid-servant, nor his ox,
nor his ass, nor any thing that is thy neighbour's.

They are most often called the Ten Commandments. But
in Jewish life, they are the אֲשֶׂרֶת הַדְּבָרִים , the Ten Words. The
classic text in the Torah supports this terminology:

> And he (Moses) was there with the Lord 40 days and 40
> nights; he did neither eat bread, nor drink water. And he
> wrote upon the tables the *words* of the covenant, the
> *ten words.*"[1]

The Ten Words As a Moral System

The name "Ten Commandments" conveys obligation. The
designation "Ten Words" connotes something broader, such
as a moral system. As I have explained in the previous chapter,
an adequate moral system must include both a moral
principle and moral rules.

The Ten Words manifest all the flexibility of a moral
system. Unfortunately, some writers regard them as inflexible
"rule-book" morality. Joseph Fletcher approves the com-
ment of a stone cutter in a cartoon who, seeing Moses
holding the stone tablets, remarks to him "Aaron said
perhaps you'd let us reduce them to 'Act responsibly in
love.' "[2] For Fletcher, moral laws are to be kept sternly in
their place.[3] Love is the only binding principle of Christian
ethics.[4] In this view, the Ten Words are part of a legalistic

system which is unresponsive to the complexity of situations.

Fletcher believes that the Ten Words are a series of moral rules and therefore, by themselves, they are inadequate as a basis for morality. I will try to demonstrate that the Ten Words are far from a system of equal and rigid moral laws. They contain both a moral principle, usable as a standard for decision in difficult cases, and moral rules which, properly understood, permit exceptions.

The One-Eight Hypothesis

The Ten Words are usually divided into two tables.[5] This is the five-five division. The first table enumerates a person's duties toward God. The second table describes a person's duties to his fellow human being. I propose a different division for the purposes of ethics: the one-eight division. Let us call it the one-eight hypothesis. I perceive in the Ten Words one moral principle followed by eight moral rules. The Ten Words, thus, constitute the fundamentals of a moral system.

What is the moral principle in the Ten Words? Can we find in them something comparable to the golden rule or the categorical imperative or the utilitarian principle? To discover it, we do not need to look beyond the second word: "Thou shalt have no other gods before Me." This principle is a source of moral rules and does not admit of exceptions. We are always called upon to resist idolatry—to keep our priorities straight by not making power, wealth, prestige or anything else but obedience to God our primary goal and fundamental loyalty. When faced with an ethical choice, we must ask: "Am I being loyal to God? Or am I obeying my nation, my social group, my selfish desires?" This is the principle of priorities.

This principle cannot be separated from the first word which describes God as the redeemer from slavery. For the first word, with its emphasis on freedom, describes the kind of God who demands our loyalty. This is a God who cares, an ethical God. To such a God, we owe obedience. For the purposes of ethics, the first and second words are inseparable.

Together, they form a compelling moral expression of ethical monotheism.

Words three through ten are moral rules. Since they are rules, not principles, we can find exceptions to each. Earlier in this book, I quoted the case of Mrs. Bergmeier which constituted an exception to the Seventh Word. The Maccabees (Jewish freedom fighters of the 2nd century B.C.E.) violated the Sabbath in order to preserve Judaism. Occasionally, there are truly sadistic parents who should not be honoured. In some situations, stealing is justified. And so it is for every word.

The Sixth Word

The sixth word: "Thou shalt not murder," may present a special difficulty. Some may argue that even if every other word from three through ten is a moral rule, surely this sixth word permits no exceptions and is a moral principle.

What is the correct translation of לא תרצח , the sixth commandment? "Thou shalt not kill," is the King James translation. "Thou shalt not murder," is the Jewish Publication Society rendition. Neither translation is completely accurate. The King James version falters because the English verb, "to kill," is far broader in meaning than the Hebrew verb, רצח . The prohibition, "Thou shalt not kill," rules out a wide spectrum of acts including those of legitimate self defense. The Hebrew original has no such intention. Any attempt, therefore, to base a claim of conscientious objection to military service on the sixth word is not justified by the Hebrew text. The Jewish Publication Society translation, "Thou shalt not murder," on the other hand, is too narrow. For the Hebrew לא תרצח goes beyond premeditated (first degree), and intentional but not premeditated (second degree) murder to include unintentional killing (manslaughter).[6] Thus, the Hebrew phrase לא תרצח prohibits not only the malicious, but even the careless destruction of human life. It applies, among other things, to such modern instruments of manslaughter as mercury poisoning caused by the irresponsible discharge of industrial wastes into waters which flow into fishing grounds.

In the previous chapter, I mentioned as one of the less

44

comprehensive moral principles, the principle that killing for the sake of killing is always wrong. The sixth word obviously covers much more territory than this moral principle. The moral principle has no exceptions, but I believe the sixth word does—certain cases of euthanasia, for example. Perhaps murder would be justified in the case of a man in agony who is hopelessly caught in the burning wreckage of a plane and pleads to be shot. In regard to manslaughter we can certainly conceive of a group required to use, for its defense, dangerous weapons such as land mines which could cause fatal accidents. Despite these exceptions, the sixth word remains the deepest of the moral rules, the closest to essential morality. It rightly heads the second tablet. It should be set aside only with supreme reluctance.

The Ten Words are a well balanced moral system containing a guiding moral principle and incisive moral rules. The principle is everywhere and always valid. The moral rules permit exceptions. Guided by the moral principle a person seeking the right choice will hopefully distinguish between true and false exceptions to the rule.

Jewish Tradition and the One-eight Hypothesis

On the first appearance, the one-eight division of the Ten Words may seem surprising. But there is some traditional support for this hypothesis. Indeed, the idea is implicit in the traditional Jewish commentaries.

Many commentators have noted that the first and second words speak of God in the first person, while the remaining words refer to God in the third person. The commentators conclude that only the first two words were spoken to the people directly by God.[7] Thus the first two words, the ones spoken by God, achieve a special prominence.

Furthermore, in rabbinic literature, the first word is often interpreted in terms of the second as a prohibition against idolatry.[8] In an unpublished thesis, William Rudolph writes:

A large number of midrashim, when taken as a whole, give us the unmistakable impression that the first

45

commandment was often considered by the rabbis to be synonymous with the second. In other words, the two are considered to be interchangeable warnings against idolatry.[9]

There is, thus, a measure of rabbinic support for the one-eight hypothesis. In one passage, the prohibition of idolatry is called in a figure of speech "as weighty as all the others."[10] Certainly, in terms of Jewish history, this has been the great operative principle of the people Israel. The myth of Abraham breaking the idols is the reality of Jewish experience. The Jew has been the great dissenter of history, a dissent born out of an unyielding commitment to the second word.

What then, is the status of the first word? Is it simply, for the purposes of ethics, absorbed into and utilized by the second? No, it achieves independent status as the authority for the Ten Words. This is what we would expect on the basis of similar covenant forms found in Hittite treaties[11] prior to and contemporaneous with the Ten Words and also from rabbinic interpretation.[12] But this authority is not just any authority. It is an authority inseparable from goodness. It is the authority of a God who cares about freedom. The authority for a moral system can only proceed from a moral source. Only an ethical God can appeal to the conscience of a human being.

Although there is considerable support in Jewish tradition for understanding the first two words in their ethical sense as a single moral principle, it would be unfair to claim traditional approval for the idea that words three through ten are moral rules. A famous passage in the Talmud argues that the commandments prohibiting murder and adultery permit no exceptions, and death is to be preferred to setting them aside.[13] Thus, in effect, the Talmud understood the sixth and seventh words as moral principles. I disagree, and I believe that the examples I have cited and the distinctions I have drawn demonstrate the validity of the one-eight hypothesis.

Firmness in the Ten Words—What Is a Moral Rule?

As a moral system, the Ten Words reveal a perhaps unexpected flexibility. But they retain a firmness necessary for the moral life. Of course, they have the stability which a universal moral principle brings. But there is another type of firmness in them which we can discover if we investigate more carefully the nature of a moral rule.

To Fletcher, rules are illuminators, but not directors. They must be kept in a subservient place. Only love and reason really count in the crunch.[14] Fletcher writes:

> One competent situationist, speaking to students, explained the position this way. Rules are like "punt on fourth down," or "Take a pitch when the count is three balls." These rules are part of the wise player's know how, and distinguish him from the novice. But they are not unbreakable. The best players are those who know when to ignore them.[15]

Thus, rules are, for Fletcher, only guidelines. Such guidelines surely have little power to compel.

One of the most incisive articles in modern ethical theory will help us to clarify the nature of a moral rule. In his article, "Two Concepts of Rules," John Rawls distinguishes between summary rules and practice rules. Summary rules are guidelines, rules of thumb, based on past experience. They are summaries of proper types of action based on experience.[16] Thus, they do not compel. Practice rules are quite different. Such a rule defines a practice like promising. There can be no practice without the rules which determine its nature.[17] Thus, practice rules cannot be lightly set aside, for they are integral to the activity in question. Rawls explains:

> The point is illustrated by the behaviour expected of a player in games. If one wants to play a game, one doesn't treat the rules of the game as guides as to what is best in particular cases. In a game of baseball if a

batter were to ask, "Can I have four strikes?" it would be assumed that he was asking what the rule was; and if, when told what the rule was, he were to say that he meant on this occasion he thought it would be best on the whole for him to have four strikes rather than three, this would be most kindly taken as a joke.[18]

To keep a promise, for example, must be more than a summary rule. A person cannot break a promise and then simply say that he felt breaking it was best on the whole. Such a person does not understand what promising is all about. For the purpose of promising is to set aside in advance such prudential considerations so the future may be secured and plans made. Rawls says, "The promisor is bound because he promised: weighing the case on its merits is not open to him."[19] There are exceptional reasons for not keeping a promise, but surely one cannot argue that keeping a promise is only a rule of prudence and may be dispensed with when the promisor feels it is wise on the whole to do so. Keeping a promise is a practice rule, not a summary or prudential rule.

Punt on fourth down is a summary rule. Three strikes and you're out is a practice rule. Keeping a promise is a practice rule. A practice rule compels in a way a summary rule does not. The distinction between these two kinds of rules is essential to the understanding of what a moral rule really is.

Moral rules are practice rules, not summary rules.[20] "Thou shalt not commit adultery," for example, is more than a rule of prudence. It penetrates to the heart of the marital commitment. For marriage means that two people have made a covenant and set themselves aside for each other.

The moral rules of the Ten Words are practice rules. The prohibition of stealing is essential to the institution of property. The prohibition of false witness is essential to the institution of law. The prohibition of murder is essential to the institution of society itself. The honoring of parents is essential to the institution of the family. It also seems essential in a human being's relationship to God that he speak of God carefully and that he set aside a fixed time for worship and meditation.

Moral rules thus have a binding power. They obligate because they are essential to the practice or institution they define. It is this binding power of the moral rule which is captured in the terse, strong, words: "Thou shalt not." Moral rules do have exceptions. But they are, nevertheless, compelling and deeply rooted.

Moral rules are essential to the institutions they define. If there were no obligation to keep a promise, there could be no institution of promising. And if there were no institutions such as promising, or marriage, or respect for property, human relationships would deteriorate. We thus return to the definition of a moral law—a moral law expresses the ethical interactions necessary to constructive human relationships. A moral rule is not a guideline, it is an obligation rooted in the structure of the human relationship.

Although exceptions to moral rules are sometimes justified, even these justified exceptions have harmful results. In the previous chapter, I argued that in a society where mutual suspicion and hostility prevail, where truth telling is dangerous in the extreme, the rule against lying may have to be set aside. The rule of truth telling does not obligate in such a situation, but it still applies and has consequences. There is no doubt that the quality of human relationships deteriorates in a pervasive climate of lying.

Just how indispensible moral rules are to the survival of a humane society can best be seen if we invert once again, as we did in the first chapter of this book, the last five of the Ten Words:

> Thou shalt murder
> Thou shalt commit adultery
> Thou shalt steal
> Thou shalt bear false witness against thy
>   neighbour
> Thou shalt covet.

The importance and the binding power of moral rules should now be clear.

The Sequence of the Ten Words

I have discussed the Ten Words as a moral system beginning with an exalted moral principle followed by eight powerful moral rules. A closer examination of the sequence of the Ten Words will further demonstrate their character as a moral system. Such an examination finds in them a general (although not perfect)[21] progression from the abstract to the concrete. The first and second words speak of the invisible God who cannot be made visible. The third and fourth words also refer to the unseen, to the name and time. The fifth word focuses on persons, specifically on the older generation. This is the humanization of time. For nothing makes the passage of time so real to us as the aging and death of our parents. The sixth and seventh words move further into the concrete, speaking of human life itself and the holiest of life's relationships, marriage. With the eighth word, we enter the very physical world of property. The ninth word brings us into the conflicts of the court of law, and involves questions of fact and truth. The false witness may endanger the life, property, and reputation of the accused. The tenth word speaks in lingering detail of those things which belong to my neighbor. Nothing is so concrete as the object we crave and intrigue to possess. For it should be understood that the Hebrew word we translate as "covet," means, in fact, not only a passionate desiring, but also the action of intriguing to possess.[22] The progression in the ten words is, thus, from the invisible God to the richly physical object of desire. Since a moral principle is by its nature more abstract than a moral rule,[23] the very arrangement of the Ten Words tends to confirm my belief that they are a moral system.

Religion and Ethics Inseparable

If we understand them as a moral system, it makes little difference whether we call them Ten Words or Ten Commandments. A Jew, however, must on some occasions, at least, use the designation Ten Words, because for him they are more than a moral system. They are the conditions of the covenant between God and Israel.[24] They are, thus, ethics in the context of a covenant relationship. Such an ethic we may call covenant ethics.

In covenant ethics in particular, and in Judaism in general, the religious and the ethical are inseparable. The awesome religious experience has an enduring ethical content. Mount Sinai was covered with smoke, but "Thou shalt not" was heard.[25] The noblest ethical teaching has a powerful religious dimension: "Thou shalt love thy neighbor as thyself: I am the Lord."[26]

Religion and ethics inseparable! In every single word there is both the duty to God and the duty to persons. The first two words proclaim the authority and sovereignty of God. But they also commend freedom and establish priorities. The third word proscribes the misuse of God's name. But it also involves, in the making of an oath, the obligation to keep our promises. The fourth word sets aside the seventh day for God, but the man servant, the maid servant, the stranger and the cattle must share in it. Parents are the subject of the fifth word, but God is remembered as the ultimate giver. Then comes that powerful series of ethical commands, four staccato imperatives and then the concluding fifth, behind each word the authority of a commanding God. Each word is religious. Each word is ethical. A human being and God meet on a bridge of Ten Words.

The Importance of the Ten Words
The Ten Words are the fundamentals of a moral system. A system of genuine flexibility which combines a comprehensive moral principle with specific moral rules in order to meet the tangled situations of life. And yet, this moral system has all the firmness which incisive moral rules can provide. For moral rules are more than guidelines accumulated from past experience. They are laws expressive of the ethical connections necessary to constructive human relationships.

Nowhere else, in the ancient or modern world, can there be found so concise, so comprehensive, so compelling a moral system. The Ten Words resist the primitive arrogance, hate, lust and greed which are still so much a part of humankind. That great series of prohibitions struggles against all that is

51

destructive within us. What, among other things, marks the line between humane civilization and the jungle? Two tablets and ten words—these are the boundary stones and the markers.

In a conversation in his Berlin apartment in 1937, Hitler turned from a general assault on Judaism and Christianity to a specific attack on the Ten Words:

It is not merely a question of Christianity and Judaism. We are fighting against the most ancient curse that humanity has brought upon itself. We are fighting against the perversion of our soundest instincts. Ah, the God of the deserts, that crazed, stupid, vengeful Asiatic despot with his powers to make laws! That slavekeeper's whip! That devilish "Thou shalt, thou shalt!" And that stupid, "Thou shalt not." It's got to get out of our blood, that curse from Mount Sinai! That poison with which both Jews and Christians have spoiled and soiled the free, wonderful instincts of man and lowered them to the level of doglike fright...Whatever is against nature is against life itself. That's why nations die out. They kill themselves under the curse of that "Thou shalt" and "Thou shalt not."

Goebbels interrupted: "Honor thy father and thy mother? No! Every boy revolts, and hates his father, and must do so to start his own life. It's an immortal law of nature."

Hitler's voice was loud in the small room: "Thou shalt not steal? Wrong! All life is theft."

Goebbels laughed derisively as he said: "Thou shalt not desire thy neighbor's this and that...Thou shalt not commit adultery...Thou shalt, thou shalt not...what not."

Hitler concluded the attack: "I am the Lord thy God! Who? That Asiatic tyrant? No! The day will come when I shall hold up against these commandments the tables of a new law. And history will recognize our movement as the great battle for humanity's liberation, a liberation from the curse of Mount Sinai, from the dark stam-

52

merings of nomads who could no more trust their own sound instincts, who could understand the divine only in the form of a tyrant who orders one to do the very things one doesn't like. This is what we are fighting against: the masochistic spirit of self-torment, the curse of so-called morals, idolized to protect the weak from the strong in the face of the immortal law of battle, the great law of divine nature. Against the so-called ten commandments, against them we are fighting." [27]

Such was the "liberation" from the Ten Words which drenched the earth in blood.

NOTES

1. Exodus 34:28. Italics mine.

2. Joseph Fletcher, *Situation Ethics*, Philadelphia: Westminster, 1966, p. 28.

3. ibid p. 55.

4. ibid p. 30.

5. J. H. Hertz, *The Pentateuch and Haftorahs*. London: Soncino, 1965, p. 295.

6. Stamm and Andrew, *The Ten Commandments in Recent Research*. Naperville, Illinois: Alec R. Allenson, 1967, pp. 98, 99.

7. Babylonian Talmud, Makkot 23b-24a.

8. Babylonian Talmud, Gittin 57b.

9. William O. Rudolph, "A Study of Rabbinic Commentary to the Ten Commandments." M.A.H.L. thesis, Hebrew Union College, p. 42. A midrash is a rabbinic interpretation of a biblical passage. Midrashim is the plural of midrash.

10. Babylonian Talmud, Horayot 8a.

11. George E. Mendenhall, "Covenant Forms in Israelite Tradition," *The Biblical Archaeologist:* September, 1954, (Vol. 17, No. 3) p. 58.

12. Jacob Z. Lauterbach, Mekilta. Philadelphia: Jewish Publication Society, 1949, Vol. 2, pp. 229, 230. (Tractate Bahodesh, Chapter 5).

13. Babylonian Talmud, Sanhedrin 74a. The passage reads: "Rabbi Johanan said in the name of Rabbi Simeon ben Jehozadak: By a majority vote, it was resolved in the upper chambers of the house of Nithza in Lydda that in every (other) law of the Torah, if a man is commanded: 'Transgress and suffer not death' he may transgress and not suffer death, excepting idolatry, incest (which includes adultery), and murder." This passage and the subsequent discussion presents, on the whole, a strict view concerning exceptions and it would surely rule out the cases of Mrs. Bergmeier and the man dying in the burning plane.

14. Joseph Fletcher, p. 31.

15. ibid p. 28.

16. In Philippa Foot, ed., *Theories of Ethics*. United States: Oxford University, 1967. p. 158.

17. ibid pp. 162, 163.

18. ibid p. 164.

19. ibid p. 156.

20. Rawls, suprisingly, considering his extended discussion of promise keeping as a practice rule, feels that most *moral rules* (italics his) are not practice rules. He fails to see the implications of his previous arguments. Rawls expresses his feeling in a footnote, but does not argue it. See ibid p. 170.

21. The fourth word is more abstract than the third. But the third follows naturally from the first and second. The ninth word is more abstract than the eighth, even if the eighth originally referred, as Stamm believed, to kidnapping. The ninth word, however, does take us into the concreteness of human conflicts as they develop in a community.

22. See Stamm and Andrew, p. 103.

23. A. I. Melden, p. 169.

24. See Exodus 34:27, 28.

25. Exodus 19:16-18.

26. Leviticus 19:18.

27. In Armin L. Robinson, ed., *The Ten Commandments*, New York: Simon and Schuster, 1943, pp. XII, XIII.

Chapter V
THE GOLDEN COMMANDMENT AND THE GOLDEN RULE

No other moral principle is so direct and powerful as the golden rule. In the first century B.C.E., the sage Hillel stated the rule in its negative form, "What is hateful unto you, do not do unto thy neighbor."[1] A few decades later, Jesus gave it a positive formulation, "Whatever you wish that men would do to you, do so to them."[2]

The Golden Commandment

A sentence found in verse eighteen of the nineteenth chapter of Leviticus is the source, for Jews and Christians, of the golden rule.[3] The entire verse reads: "Thou shalt not take vengeance, nor bear any grudge against the children of thy people, but thou shalt love thy neighbor as thyself: I am the Lord." This short Hebrew sentence, וְאָהַבְתָּ לְרֵעֲךָ כָּמוֹךָ "Thou shalt love thy neighbor as thyself," is the source of the golden rule, and I call it the golden commandment. It dates back to at least the sixth century B.C.E.[4]

What does the phrase "as thyself" in the golden commandment mean? Does it mean loving as much as you love yourself? Or does it mean loving as a person like yourself?

A careful translation of the Hebrew text clarifies the issue. The word in question is כָּמוֹךָ (kamokha). Leo Baeck pointed out that כָּמוֹךָ (kamokha) despite the fact that it is usually translated "as thyself" is not, as we might think, reflexive. Baeck translated the phrase, "he is as thou."[5] Sheldon Blank, Professor of Bible at the Hebrew Union College—Jewish Institute of Religion, makes the same judgment. He understands כָּמוֹךָ (kamokha) to be in a sort of appositive relationship with רֵעֲךָ (re'akha) your neighbor, a person like you.[6] The comparable uses in the Bible of this prepositional form strongly favor the interpretations of Baeck and Blank. The recently published New English Bible also concurs. It translates the clause in question, "You shall love your neighbor as a man like yourself."[7] In agreement with Baeck, Blank and the New English Bible, I would translate the golden commandment, "You shall love your neighbor as a person like yourself.'. The golden rule with its assumption of human similarity thus follows directly from the golden commandment.

Hillel and the Golden Rule

It is now clear what Hillel did when he formulated the golden rule: "What is hateful unto you, do not do unto thy neighbor." Hillel's rule leaves unsaid what is stated in the golden commandment. Hillel's golden rule does not express the command to love the neighbor; nor does it state the conviction that the neighbor is a person like yourself. While these assertions remain part of the golden rule, they are unspoken. On the other hand, Hillel made explicit what was implicit in the golden commandment. For if we are commanded to love the neighbor, and, if the neighbor is a person similar to ourselves, then it follows that what is hateful to us will be hateful to him; and we should refrain from doing it. By restating the golden commandment so as to make its consequences explicit, Hillel made it more directly usable in the world of action.

Comparing Moral Principles—
Stages in Moral Decision Making

Now that we understand the development and meaning of the golden rule, we are ready to compare it to the other great moral principles. For the purpose of this examination, let us take a simple moral choice and describe the stages by which we arrive at a moral decision. Suppose I enter an unoccupied office and see on the desk a handsome pocket calculator which I am tempted to steal. By way of example, I will use Mill's principle of utility in arriving at a decision. This principle states: "Actions are right in proportion as they tend to promote happiness; wrong as they tend to produce the reverse of happiness."[8]

The first stage is the moral problem itself. A problem, let

us assume, I cannot solve simply. I say to myself, "Shall I steal the calculator?" In the second stage, I use the moral principle to put the problem into a new frame of reference. I ask, "Does stealing the calculator promote the general happiness?" In the third stage, I make a judgment of fact as to the effect of the act (or acts) in question in the new frame of reference. This judgment more fully describes the projected situation. I say, "I am depriving another human being of a possession he values and diminishing the level of trust in my society. I am decreasing the general happiness." In the fourth stage, I react to that judgment of fact. My reaction is shaped by my spontaneous response as a human being to the projected situation and to the values endangered in it. I certainly do not want to diminish the general happiness. I say to myself, "I wouldn't like that." In the fifth and final stage, I use the moral principle to make a decision. I may still be tempted to steal the calculator, but having visualized and reacted to the consequences of immoral action, I am more than ever committed to moral behavior and, using the moral principle as my guide, can now make a moral choice. Since I cannot will to diminish the general happiness, I say to myself with conviction, "It is not right. I will not steal the calculator."

There are, thus, five stages in the process of moral decision making with the help of principles. They are: the moral problem, the new frame of reference, the judgment of fact, the reaction to the judgment of fact, and the moral decision. I have used the example of decision making with the help of the principle of utility. It is relatively simple to apply the other principles. The second word fits the pattern exactly. The golden rule shortens the process in a way I will soon explain. The categorical imperative, as Kant used it, requires some explanation.

The categorical imperative states: "Act only according to that maxim by which you can at the same time will that it should be a universal law."[9] Thus in creating a new frame of reference, I ask, "What would happen if everyone in similar circumstances stole a calculator?" I am now ready for the judgment of fact. On an intellectual level a conflict emerges: I seek to possess the calculator yet my very act of theft undermines the institution of private property. On a more practical level I realize that if everyone in similar circumstances stole a calculator, no one's calculator, including my own, would be safe. The next stage is the reaction to the judgment of fact. On an intellectual level I balk at an internal contradiction: it is absurd to both wish to "own" and to undermine the institution of "owning." But on a more practical level I realize that I do not want to live in a world where no one's calculator, including my own, would be safe. The final stage is the moral decision. I determine not to steal the calculator since I cannot will that calculator stealing be a universal law of action.

The categorical imperative fits the pattern of moral decision making I have described. For the purposes of this book I will utilize the categorical imperative only as it operates on the practical level.[10]

STAGES IN MORAL DECISION MAKING
WITH THE AID OF MORAL PRINCIPLES

	The Principle of Utility	The Categorical Imperative	The Second Word	The Golden Rule
1. The Moral Problem	Shall I steal the calculator?	Shall I steal the calculator?	Shall I steal the calculator?	Shall I steal the calculator?
2. The New Frame of Reference	Does stealing the calculator promote the general happiness?	What would happen if everyone in similar circumstances stole a calculator?	Am I putting my desire for the calculator above loyalty to God?	How would I like my own calculator stolen?
3. The Judgment of Fact	I am depriving another human being of a possession he values & diminishing the level of trust in my society.	No one's calculator, including my own, would be safe.	I will be disloyal to God by breaking His commandment—Thou shalt not steal.	
4. Reaction to the Judgment of Fact	I wouldn't want to diminish the general happiness.	I wouldn't like to live in a world like that.	I wouldn't want to be disloyal to God.	I wouldn't like my own calculator stolen.
5. The Moral Decision	It is not right. I will not steal the calculator.	It is not right. I will not steal the calculator.	It is not right. I will not steal the calculator.	It is not right. I will not steal the calculator.

61

It may be instructive to examine the use of the categorical imperative in a more complex situation than the one provided by our sample problem of stealing a calculator. I will utilize a moral decision I faced in my own life. In May of 1973, at a crucial stage in the grape strike, the local organizer of the United Farm Workers asked me to travel to Coachella, California, to participate in a clergy demonstration in support of the striking migrant workers. Clergy from all over the country had been asked to take part. The timing was right—it was feasible for me to be away from my congregation for two days. The money to travel to Coachella was available in my travel fund. Therefore, it was possible for me to participate. On the negative side, there was a slight risk of physical danger. As a husband and father as well as a person who treasures his own life, I had to consider that danger. Exaggerated fears aside, the danger was minimal. Nevertheless, a certain inertia rooted me in Seattle. I certainly was busy enough and tired enough to resist a trip to Coachella. To focus the issue and come to a decision, I used the categorical imperative and asked myself: What would happen if every rabbi who was able to go to Coachella refused to make the journey? I certainly would not want rabbis absent from what I considered an important moral action. By extension, if priests and ministers likewise failed to come, the farm workers would have been deprived of clergy support indispensable to their struggle. The categorical imperative clarified the issue, and I decided to go to Coachella. It was the right decision, and the categorical imperative helped me to make it.

However, if the physical danger had been great, I do not think I would have participated. My duty to my wife and children would have outweighed my duty to the farm workers. I could still use the categorical imperative and ask myself: What would happen if everyone in similar circumstances refused to go to Coachella? There would be two major results. No clergy with small children would go to Coachella. This outcome is good, for it means that no little children of clergy would be bereaved of a parent because of the Coachella action. The second consequence is that there would be fewer clergy available to go to Coachella and less support for the farm workers at the scene of the action. This result is obviously bad. Nevertheless, those clergy without children and therefore freer to risk their lives in a noble cause might still go to Coachella. Or some other, less dangerous means would have to be found to help the farm workers. Indeed, as violence escalated that summer of 1973, Cesar Chavez, the leader of the farm workers, pulled away the picket lines and averted all confrontations in order to prevent further loss of life. I do not pretend that there is any way to take the agony out of moral decision making. But the categorical imperative, like the other great moral principles, always remains usable and helpful.

Special Attributes of the Golden Rule

The critical stage in moral decision making with the aid of moral principles is putting the problem into a new frame of reference. With the categorical imperative, we visualize the consequences of the universal practice of an action. With the principle of utility, we calculate the effect of the action on the general happiness. With the second word, we consider the effect of the action on our loyalty to God. With the golden rule, however, we consult our own experience directly. We simply say, as in the case of our sample moral problem, "How would I like my calculator stolen?"

It is clear, therefore, that the frame of reference in the golden rule is more concrete and less abstract than in the other moral principles. It is surely more concrete to make reference to my own feelings than to the general happiness.

The operation of the golden rule is also more direct than that of the other principles. Since the new frame of reference is my own feeling, we do not need to first analyze the effect of the action on, for example, the general security of property, before we return to my reaction. We are already there. Once I have said, "How would I like my own calculator stolen?" I need make no further judgments. I immediately respond in the negative and then use the golden rule to make a moral decision not to steal the calculator. Stage three—the judgment of the effects of the action—has been eliminated.

The golden rule is, therefore, both more concrete and more direct than the other moral principles. It, thus, requires less capacity for abstract and extended thought. This is the golden rule's unique power. It is so basic to life that all ages and manner of persons can be moved by it. My three-year-old daughter can understand that, just as she would not like her parents to devour all the cookies leaving none for herself, so she should not eat up all the cookies, leaving none for her parents.

The golden rule is also especially powerful in its capacity to elicit a moral choice in the final stage of decision making. It persuades me to think of my neighbor as a person like myself. It even stirs me to realize that he has feelings like mine. A human bond is forged, and that bond is not only intellectual; it is on the deeper level of feelings. Thus, in the moment of decision, the golden rule has done more than tell me what is right. It has connected me with my neighbor emotionally. It is, thus, much harder for me to pursue my own advantage at his expense.

The second word can also elicit moral behavior in the final stage of decision making, for it reminds us of our loyalty to God. To fail is to betray the purpose of our lives. I may still want to steal the calculator of our sample moral problem, but I want even more to remain loyal to God. The utilitarian principle is, in my judgment, generally less powerful in compelling moral behavior. The motivation for obedience to it, as John Stuart Mill argued, is, "the social feelings of mankind—the desire to be in unity with our fellow creatures."[11] Unhappily, "the social feelings of mankind," are not, at this stage in evolution, very well developed. Individuals and groups are all too willing to sacrifice the needs of others for their own advantage. The categorical imperative can be quite potent in eliciting moral behavior, especially if it is understood in such a way as to call into question the order and reliability of the kind of humane society any sensible person desires to live in. In that case, it demonstrates the chaos which can open up under our feet and, thus, may shock us into the necessity for moral behavior.

The golden rule has some special attributes. It is concrete; it is direct; and it, above all other principles, builds the human connections which moral principles are formulated to defend. It is a principle of spectacular simplicity and beauty.

A Substantial Objection to the Golden Rule

The golden rule is a basic moral principle. But is it a principle without qualification? Does it hold in all circumstances?

There is only one substantial objection to the golden rule.[12] Whenever differences are the significant factor in a relationship, it does not apply. For then what is hateful to one person may not indeed be hateful to another. And what one person desires for himself, another may not wish for himself. When the assumptions of similarity which are the basis of the golden rule no longer hold, the rule itself no longer applies. Thus, an athletic father may be wrong in forcing his non-athletic son to play football. Or a western culture may be wrong to inflict its way of life on an eastern culture. Or, to use a trivial example, a wife who dislikes rare meat would be wrong to refuse to cook her husband's meat rare. Leonard Russell has wisely pointed out that the golden rule works best in homogeneous societies where there are not "wide differences of point of view and taste and need...."[13] For those relationships in which difference is the significant factor, we shall have to find a principle other than the golden rule to clarify and instruct our behavior.

We should not be surprised to discover that even great laws are limited in the scope of their application. Once again, the laws of physics will serve as a useful analogy. Newtonian mechanics works on the macroscopic scale. Quantum mechanics works on the atomic and sub-atomic scale. An even more evocative analogy, however, involves the principle of complementarity. In some situations, light acts like a wave with its energy spread out evenly over a wide front. In other situations, light acts like photons which are lumps of energy localized in small and discrete regions. There are, thus, two theories of light—the wave theory and the photon theory. Both are based on strong experimental evidence. Neither can be surrendered. The principle of complementarity maintains that both theories are true. Just as light behaves according to different theories in different situations, so also the individual in some relationships will use the golden rule to act constructively; and in other relationships, he will use another, as yet undisclosed, moral principle in order to behave helpfully.

Summary—the Status of the Golden Rule

We are now ready to define the status of the golden rule. The golden rule is one of the four basic principles of morality. But its scope is less inclusive than the categorical imperative, the second word, and the principle of utility. However, its realm is far more inclusive than such moral principles as killing for the sake of killing is always wrong. Unlike moral rules which were defined in chapter three, the golden rule admits of no exceptions. Within its scope, it can never be set aside. The golden rule, is, thus, sui generis, unique. It is as deep as the other great moral principles. While not as inclusive as these, it is yet far broader in its application than what we have called the less comprehensive moral principles.

The Foundations of Morality

Thus, we have at the foundations of morality, four basic principles. One, the golden rule, is less inclusive than the other three. After these principles, we have less comprehensive principles such as, killing for the sake of killing is always wrong, stealing for the sake of stealing is always wrong, and so on. After these less comprehensive principles, we have moral rules, such as thou shalt nor murder, thou shalt not commit adultery, keep your promises, tell the truth, and others. After these moral rules, there all kinds of standards and customs. Examples would be standards regarding premarital sexual intercourse or customs relating to appropriate dress.

What Is the Common Theme?

In each of the great moral principles, the frame of

reference differs. In one, we consider the consequences of universal practice; in another, the influence on the general happiness; in another, the effect on our loyalty to God; and in another, our response to such an action done to ourselves. The frame of reference differs, but a common theme unites all four great principles. What is that common theme?

The categorical imperative confronts us with the question, "What if everyone in similar circumstances were to do that?" This question prevents us from making an exception of ourselves. We cannot mistreat our fellow human being by setting ourselves above the moral law. The principle of utility poses the question, "Does this act promote the general happiness?" We are, thus brought beyond calculations of our own advantage and must consider the rights of all persons to a share of happiness. The golden rule asks the most direct question of all, "How would I like that done to me?" We are, thus, placed on the same level of value as our neighbor. Since the other is a human being similar to myself, I should not set myself above him to pursue my advantage at his expense. The second word forces us to ask, "Am I putting self or group ahead of loyalty to God?" This question recalls us to our primary duty—our duty to God. Then we are unable to put our selfish desires above the rights of others whom God loves and protects through the agency of moral laws established for the defense of all.

Here is the common theme which unites all four basic moral principles. It can be briefly stated: No one is above the human level, and no one is below the human level. This is the bedrock of ethics; the heart of the moral law.

Dehumanizing the Victim

Because the moral law is so clear, the savageries of history require a dehumanization of the victim. In our hearts, most of us know that to murder a fellow human being is wrong. But what if the enemy is less than human? What if the victim is below the level which merits human consideration? Thus, Lieutenant Calley, commenting on the My Lai massacre stated that, "he did not feel as if he was killing humans, but rather they were the enemy with whom one could not speak or reason."[14] Similarly, the leader of a group of Colombian cowboys who massacred 16 nomadic Indians in the prairies east of the Andes Mountains commented, "For me, Indians are animals like deer or iguanas, except the deer don't damage our crops or kill our pigs. Since way back, Indian hunting has been common practice in these parts."[15]

The Essence of the Moral Law

It is interesting to note that in the Sifra, a rabbinic commentary to the Book of Leviticus, there is a discussion concerning the greatest principle in the Torah.[16] Rabbi Akiba argued that it was the golden commandment: "Thou shalt love thy neighbor as thyself."[17] But another rabbi, Ben Azzai, found an even greater principle. He quoted the sentence, "This is the book of the generations of Adam."[18] The Torah, therefore, belongs to all persons. Its affirmation of human value, its insistence on human duty, comprehend all humanity. Ben Azzai, in selecting this verse, penetrated to the core of the moral law.

No one is above the human level and no one is below the humal level. Each is bound by duties and protected by rights. No one is above the moral laws which bind all. No one is below the moral laws which protect all. No one should step beyond right and wrong. No one should count for less than a human being. Here, in eight words, is the essence of the moral law: All persons are obligated. All persons are precious.[19]

NOTES

1. Babylonian Talmud, Shabbat 31a.

2. Matthew 7:12.

3. J. H. Hertz, *The Pentateuch and Haftorahs*. London: Soncino, 1965, p. 502.

4. Robert H. Pfeiffer, *Introduction to the Old Testament*. New York: Harper and Brothers, 1941, pp. 239 ff.

5. Leo Baeck. The Dr. Samuel Schulman Lectures at the Hebrew Union College—Jewish Institute of Religion. "The Interrelation of Judaism and Ethics." Cincinnati: 1949, p. 20.

6. Letter from Sheldon Blank to Norman Hirsh. April 8, 1972.
   "About loving your neighbor, there is in fact a modern translation that does avoid the reflexive. The New English Bible renders it: 'You shall love your neighbor as a man like yourself,' which seems to me to be pretty good. I do think כמוך goes with לרעך in a sort of appositive relationship: "Your neighbor, a person like you." I would compare Genesis 44:15 איש אשר כמני or Judges 8:18: כמוך כמהם or Job 12:3: כמוכם אנכי נפל לא, especially the Genesis passage. To be sure, one could justify the interpretation of כמוך as reflexive by comparing Jeremiah 7:19: הַלֹא אֹתָם לְמַעַן בֹּשֶׁת פְּנֵיהֶם where אתם לא is elliptical for אתם מכעסים הם in contrast to הַמֹּתִי אֹתִי הֵם Similarly, one might say, the כמוך in the Leviticus passage is elliptical for אֹהֵב אֶת עַצְמְךָ in comparison with וְאָהַבְתָּ But I prefer the appositive: 'a person like you.' "

7. The New English Bible, The Old Testament. The United States of America: Oxford University Press, Cambridge University Press, 1970, p. 156.

8. Smith and Sosa, *Mill's Utilitarianism*, Belmont, California: Wadsworth, 1969, p. 36

9. Immanuel Kant, *Foundations of the Metaphysics of Morals*. Indianapolis and New York: Bobbs - Merrill, 1959, p. 39.

10. Kant distinguishes between two types of duties: perfect and imperfect. Perfect duties are more compelling. They involve the rights of others. Kant uses the example of keeping our promises.

To promise and intend not to keep the promise is a contradiction, for if everyone did that the institution of promising would be undermined. Imperfect duties do not involve the rights of others. These duties are connected with benevolence. Kant uses the example of charity to those in need. There is no inherent contradiction if everyone cared only about himself and refused to give charity. However, we cannot will that this be a universal practice because such a practice would deprive us, in our time of need, of the help we desire.

While Kant argues in regard to perfect duties that when we seek to universalize their violation we encounter an internal contradiction, it is clear that violations of perfect duties (like violations of imperfect duties) involve a conflict with our will. Just as we do not want to live in a world without charity, so we do not want to live in a world where promises are not kept.

I believe a careful reading of Kant supports my contention: He wrote: "Some actions are of such a nature that their maxim cannot even be thought as a universal law of nature without contradiction, far from it being possible that one could will that it should be such. In others this internal impossibility is not found, though it is still impossible to will that their maxim should be raised to the Universality of a law of nature, because such a will would contradict itself." Immanuel Kant, *Foundations of the Metaphysics of Morals.* Indianapolis and New York: Bobbs - Merrill, 1959, pp. 41, 42.

Stealing a calculator is a violation of a perfect duty—the right of another is involved. In the chart on page 61 I do not refer to the internal contradiction involved in the violation of a perfect duty, e.g. the nullification of private property, for this is an intellectual consideration. Rather, I stress the practical consideration that we cannot will to live in a world where violations of a perfect duty prevail, e.g. where theft becomes a universal practice. Absurdity is not a threat; chaos is. Whether we speak of perfect or imperfect duties, the true strength of the categorical imperative as a guide to decision making is revealed only when we ask the practical question of how we would like to live in a world where a particular violation of the moral law rules as a universal practice.

11. Smith and Sosa, *Mill's Utilitarianism*, Belmont, California: Wadsworth, 1969, p. 58.

12. I do not consider the objections based on a literal reading of the rule to be substantive. In such objections, the positive version of the rule is easier to use and therefore preferred. On such a literal

reading, one could argue that a person might wish for the cooperation of another in crime and be willing to recompense it. Or that a masochist who wanted to be tortured would be commanded to torture others. Or that a quarrelsome person who loves to be provoked, should go about provoking others. These literal interpretations miss the point. Any moral principle assumes a person who is willing to do what is right, at least after the consequences of immoral action are clarified for him. The persons involved in these objections to the golden rule are set and determined on a course of evil.

13. Leonard J. Russel, "Ideals and Practice (1)." In *Philisophy*, Vol. XVII, No. 66, April 1942, p. 110.

14. *The Seattle Post Intelligencer*, February 18, 1971.

15. *Time Magazine*, July 10, 1972, p. 33.

16. Sifra, 89b.

17 Leviticus 19:18.

18 Genesis 5:1.

19. The essence of the moral law can be expressed as a principle of duties and rights: Treat all persons as obligated, including yourself; treat all persons as precious, including your enemies.

This chapter has many practical applications for the encouragement of ethical behavior. A careful analysis of the five stages of moral decision making will provide insights useful to moral education. For example, putting the problem in a new frame of reference is crucial. Children could learn what are the right questions to ask when faced with a difficult moral problem. What if everyone were to do that? How would I like that done to me? Am I putting God first? Does it promote the general happiness? Of course, some of these questions will speak to some families, and others to other families. The golden rule, however, is probably the best place to begin.

When it comes to the stage of moral decision, a person can always say, "So what? So what if I do not contribute to the preservation of a humane society. So what if I do not contribute to the general happiness. So what if I am not loyal to God. So what that it would be hateful to me and it will be hateful to him. So what, I will pursue my own advantage." Thus, a commitment to the preservation of a humane society, to the general happiness, to loyalty to God, should be developed. Likewise, a bond of true care with the fellow human being needs to be created.

The essence of the great moral principles can be expressed in a few short sentences: All persons are obligated. All persons are precious. And there are no exceptions. This is the heart of ethics and it should be taught. If these few sentences can be humanized with examples and taken to heart by the student, then he will have written the moral law on his own consciousness.

It will also be helpful if the young learn respect for specific moral laws. Keep your promises is an important instruction to the young, although they will learn later that there are exceptions. First, however, they need to learn that moral laws are expected to be kept.

The primary task of moral education is to develop a moral self image in the young. The young person should achieve a consciousness that we become truly human not by the exercise of physical courage nor by excellence of mind, but primarily by moral actions. In the ethical life, as we have seen in previous chapters, everything ultimately depends on the moral self image.

It is for this reason that the widespread assault upon the virtue of compassion in the last twenty years—an assault which President Brewster of Yale University has brilliantly described—is dangerous. Compassion is one of the highest virtues—the Talmud even mentions it first in describing the character of the Jew. But now, compassion is in disrepute. We have another image for the human being—the tough guy. Senator Joseph McCarthy castigated the "bleeding hearts." In President Kennedy's Camelot, it was "clout" that was most honored. President Johnson could not abide the "nervous Nellies" who opposed escalation of the Vietnam War. President Nixon believed in "toughing it through" and glorified the ethic of professional football. But life is not a professional football game. Life requires compassion and wisdom just as much as it requires courage. Abraham Lincoln was not less a human being because he could say: "With malice toward none; with charity for all." The tough guy is one image of the human being—but it is not an image which can lead to an ethical life. Children who model themselves on tough guys will not develop a moral self image. No moral model, no moral self image. No moral self image, no moral life. If society is to remain moral, it must provide its young with exemplars of the moral life.

As children grow older, adults should explain to them the fundamental purpose of ethical actions. The causal connections between ethics and constructive human relationships and also between ethics and the growth of character can be discussed in a clear and simple way. What ethics achieves, what it contributes to, and what it does not guarantee should be clarified. The young will then not be swept into cynicism and despair when decency is repaid with evil.

These are some preliminary observations of how the theoretical discussions of this and other chapters may be applied to the task of moral education.

Chapter VI
THE FREEDOM COMMANDMENT
AND THE FREEDOM RULE

Human beings respond in certain ways. Most people don't want their loved ones murdered, their prized possessions stolen, their good name defamed. There is a fundamental human nature on which moral laws are based. If this fundamental human nature ever changed, the moral law, as we know it, would collapse.

Moral Laws Are Rooted in Human Nature

If the character of the human interaction were altered by a change in human nature even moral principles would be drastically affected. If human nature preferred the chaos of a conflict-torn and disintegrating society to the order of a cooperative and humane one, the categorical imperative would not obligate. People would ask with puzzlement: "What is the good of an orderly and humane society that I should contribute to it?" If human nature harbored no feeling of concern for the neighbor, the golden rule would fall. Persons would ask: "Why should I treat him with the same kind of consideration I want for myself?" If human nature preferred the general suffering to the general happiness, then the principle of utility would collapse. What reason would people have to promote the general happiness? If human nature believed that primary loyalty was due not to a benevolent Creator, but rather to their immediate desires, the second commandment would lose its power to compel. What reason would persons have for loyalty to God?

Moral rules, too, would be unable to sustain such an alteration in the common human core. If human nature had no desire to possess anything, then the eighth commandment, "Thou shalt not steal," would not apply. If human nature had no objection to being falsely accused and unjustly punished, then the ninth commandment, "Thou shalt not bear false witness against thy neighbor," would not obligate.

Moral laws are rooted in fundamental human nature. They are not merely ideas conceived in the minds of idealists.

Moral laws express the ethical interactions necessary to constructive human relationships. If human nature were to change, the nature of constructive relationship would have to change too. God legislated the moral law when He created human nature.

People Are Not the Same

There is a fundamental human nature, but this does not mean people are the same. We share certain basic needs and responses. For example, we all need to possess something and we do not want our possessions stolen. Nevertheless, we differ in what we want to possess, and in how we express our anger at the theft of our possessions. Along with the basic need for possession and the response to theft, variation is built into the human structure as a climate of internal and external influences. To say that we all want to possess something is an oversimplification because, in our heredity as well as in our environment, the factors making for difference already strongly exist. It is useless to contend that differences are unimportant and that we should minimize them. There is a common human nature, and it is powerful; but it does not express itself in any one way. Sometimes it takes similar forms, at other times it take dissimilar forms. We all want happiness, but happiness sometimes means different things to us.

Genetic factors start us in different directions and the dynamics of family life continue the process. No two children, even in one family, will have the same relationship to their parents.[1] In becoming human, we become different.

The influence of a particular family on a particular individual is magnified because the human being is more malleable than the other animals. Adolf Portmann, the Swiss biologist, has pointed out that in comparison with the other higher animals, the human infant is brought into the world early.[2] Not until age one does the baby attain the stage of development the young elephant or whale or dolphin, or rhesus monkey has attained at birth. The human baby is, thus, born early into a second uterus, a social uterus, which profoundly shapes him.

76

The individual is further differentiated by his nation and culture. All nations prize freedom, for example, but in the continuum of freedoms, a freedom precious to one people may be of less consequence to another. Freedom of speech is precious to us; to the Chinese, it seems far less important. We are the products of different histories, and our values are not the same. A China expert, John K. Fairbank, has commented that Americans have not begun to experience the "suffering from feudal oppression, imperialist invasion, natural disaster, and civil strife"[3] which have shaped the Chinese mind.

We should not minimize the area of difference. In fact, in our age, the scope of relationships of difference has been enlarged. There are multiple reasons for this change. As societies become increasingly complex, wide differences in values, world views, and needs emerge. In 1796, in his Farewell Address, George Washington could say of his countrymen: "With slight shades of difference, you have the same religion, manners, habits, and political principles."[4] No modern American President could make the same claim. Along with the growth of complexity, has come an increased rate of change tied to scientific method and innovation, a breaking up of traditional world views and value systems associated with a reverence for modernity, a greater willingness of groups in the face of the homogenization of popular culture to affirm their own uniqueness, and an increasing awareness of other cultures and civilizations through the rapid growth of world-wide communications. As a consequence of all these developments, the modern individual finds himself with considerable freedom to choose among differing life styles. A father could once count on his son to remain in his craft, in his town, in his value system, and in his religious group. Their relationship reflected this identity of work, life, values and traditions. Now, this identity is often largely gone. Differences occupy a far more significant place in their relationship. Therefore, the need for a moral principle more attuned to difference than the golden rule has increased.

We do not like to confront the harsh fact of difference. But it is a reality and must be acknowledged. Moreover, a full recognition of the scope of differences does not cause division between people. The different, as well as the common, can be used to achieve constructive relationships. We must now analyze the interplay of similarity and difference as they effect the use of moral laws.

Similarity, Difference, and Moral Laws

Most similarities unite; of course, some divide. We often hate in others those qualities we possess in abundant measure ourselves. A compulsive person, for example, tends to discover and abhor compulsiveness in others. Nevertheless, at the basis of every constructive relationship, there is the common bond. Without shared memories, values, and goals, there would be no positive relationship at all. Some differences are complementary. But others antagonize and divide. Accepting these antagonizing differences is necessary to constructive relationship; it is the test of our ability to relate. We can say that discovering common ground is fundamental; accepting differences is necessary. Love is the bond of the common, and the acceptance of the different.

Here we see another example of the wisdom of the Torah. For it is characteristic of the Torah to remind persons of what they share. No less than thirty-six times we are instructed not to oppress the stranger for we were strangers in the land of Egypt.[5] The appeal is to a common experience.

There are two steps in establishing a relationship. The first and natural is to seek the shared. The second and more difficult is to discover and accept differences. The more intimate our knowledge, the more the serious differences emerge. Two persons meet. At some point, they discover the deep, dividing differences. There is in this discovery a certain shock. The relationship persists if, and only if, each person feels the other has tried to understand the differences he prizes. When these differences are accepted as unconquerable fact, to be neither obscured nor patronized, the relationship can endure in its new found wholeness.

To deny differences is to reject a part of the other person precious to him. We accept him only on our terms, only as we recreate and diminish him. But he wants to be accepted with his difference. Differences, in themselves, do not divide;

it is our inability to cope with them, our failure to love the other person as himself, which finally divides. The causes of this failure lie beyond the scope of this chapter. Nevertheless, we can postulate a failure to accept ourselves with our differences from others, an inability to communicate those experiences which have created the attitudes which offend, and an inadequate recognition that we are not the measure of all persons as possible reasons for the inability to achieve constructive relationships. Differences do pose problems. Yet it is the human condition to live in a world of differences. Why? Perhaps an answer is that people were made different so that they might learn to love.

Difference and the Freedom Rule

Differences are an integral and important part of person-to-person contact. I have explained in the last chapter that the golden rule fails to cope with differences. Therefore, it cannot apply to the entire spectrum of human relationships. Can we discover a principle, as a supplement to the golden rule, which regulates our actions in circumstances where differences prevail? We can. I call this principle the freedom rule. It, like the golden rule, can be expressed in both negative and positive forms. In its negative version, the freedom rule states:

What is hateful to you, accept in another.[6]

In its positive version, the freedom rule reads:

What is desirable to you, do not impose on another.

The freedom rule has many applications. Communism is hateful to us, but if most of the people of Vietnam preferred a communist government headed by Ho Chi Minh, we should have accepted their choice. A career in music is hateful to me, but if my son chooses it, I should accept his decision. Most Americans approve of the two-party system, but that is no justification to urge or impose it on Mexico. I like to have friends visit me unannounced, but that is no reason for me to make unannounced visits on friends who place a different value on privacy.

The following chart clarifies the differences between the golden rule and the freedom rule:

79

The Golden Rule:

Negative ————————————> Negative
    What is hateful unto you   do not do unto
                                      thy neighbor.

Positive ————————————> Positive
    Whatever you wish that men   do so to them.
    would do to you

The Freedom Rule:

Negative ————————————> Positive
    What is hateful to you   accept in another.

Positive ————————————> Negative
    What is desirable to you   do not impose on
                                        another.

The Freedom Commandment

Prior commandments are the sources for both the golden and freedom rules. The golden rule is based on the golden commandment which is popularly translated: Thou shalt love thy neighbor as thyself. A more accurate translation, as explained in the last chapter, reads: You shall love your neighbor as a person like yourself. The freedom rule is also rooted in a prior commandment. I call it the freedom commandment. The freedom commandment can be popularly expressed: Love your neighbor as himself. A more accurate formulation would read: Love your neighbor as a person different from yourself.

The Freedom Rule As a Necessary Supplement

We readily perceive the way similarity and difference, the golden and the freedom rules, interact. The golden rule helps us to seek and build upon the common ground. The freedom rule assists us in discovering and accepting differences. The freedom rule is, therefore, a necessary supplement to the golden rule.

Objections to the Freedom Rule: A First Objection

Several objections to the freedom rule should be considered. Some may claim that it is too permissive. Are there no limits to acceptance? There are. Let us examine the issue of limits using the negative version of the freedom rule: What is hateful to you, accept in another. Two possible abuses of the rule readily come to mind. Suicide is hateful to me, but if my friend prefers it, I should accept his decision. Genocide is hateful to me, but if Hitler prefers it, I should not obstruct his plan. In both of these cases we have a literal reading of the freedom rule which completely disregards the essence of the moral law: All persons are obligated and all persons are precious. A similar misrepresentation of the golden rule can also be made. Let us examine two possible abuses of the positive version of the golden rule: Whatever you wish that men would to to you, do so to them. On the basis of a literal reading of this rule, a masochist would be commanded to torture others. Similarly, a quarrelsome person who loves to be provoked, should go about provoking others. These literal interpretations miss the point. Any moral principle assumes a person who is willing to do what is right, at least after the consequences of immoral action are clarified for him.

A Second Objection

A second objection to the freedom rule contends that it is unnecessary because the golden rule applies to relationships of difference. This objection has some merit. Let us consider the case of a father tempted to prevent his son from pursuing a career in music. Using the golden rule, the father may say to himself, "As I would not want to be prevented from pursuing the career of my choice, so I should not prevent my son from pursuing the career of his choice." Using this reasoning, the father has reached an ethical decision. The golden rule applies.

Despite the merit of this objection, it does not fully stand for two reasons. In the first place, the golden rule works in a relationship of difference only if it is used in a limited and special way. Earlier in this chapter, I explained that we share core needs, but that these needs express themselves sometimes in similar and sometimes in different ways. When the ways of expression are similar, the golden rule applies; when they are different, the freedom rule applies. The golden rule applies to situations in which difference is the significant factor only if it is applied to the core human need rather than to the specific action under consideration.

An example of the golden rule functioning in an area of similarity will indicate how it applies to the concrete action in question rather than to the core human need. I am tempted to interrupt a friend who is talking earnestly to me. I ask myself how I would like to be interrupted when talking earnestly to a friend. My immediate response is negative: I would not like to be interrupted. I conclude that I should not interrupt my friend. The golden rule, we notice, has been applied to the concrete act of interrupting a friend, not to the core need to be respected. If we compare with this normative operation of the golden rule, its use in relationships of difference, the divergence is marked. Let us return to the case of the father with a son bent on pursuing a career in music. The father will not arrive at an ethical decision if he applies the golden rule to the specific act—preventing his son from pursuing a career in music. If he asks himself, "How would I have liked it if my father had prevented me from pursuing a career in music?" he answers, because he abhors music as a career, it would have been a good thing to have been saved from such a misfortune. Only if he applies the golden rule to the core need of each person to decide the course of his life, will the father come to an ethical decision.

The freedom rule, on the other hand, when applied to this case of the father and his son, óperates concretely on the action under consideration and unambiguously yields a moral conclusion. As soon as we realize that the act under consideration, e.g. pursuing a career in music, falls into the category of difference between ourselves and the other person, we resolve to use the freedom rule: What is hateful to you, accept in another. We thus arrive at a moral decision, concretely and powerfully.

The golden rule works in relationships of difference only if it is used in a special and limited way—a way in which it loses

82

concreteness and much of the effectiveness it was developed from the golden commandment to achieve. In these relationships, the golden rule is especially subject to misuse. The reason it applies at all in such situations is that, as I have explained, the common and the different are inseparable: even in the realm of differences, we can penetrate to basic common needs.

For another reason, too, the golden rule does not adequately apply to relationships of difference. The proper world of the golden rule is that of similarity and it functions by the process of identification. This is clearly understood if we analyze the two parts of the rule. First, the golden rule serves as a general principle of value. It instructs us not to do what is hateful to our neighbor. Second, it functions as a specific standard of judgment. It determines what, in fact, will be hateful to our neighbor. We are the standard. What is hateful to us, will be hateful to him. Thus, when wide differences prevail, it breaks down because, as Leonard Russell argued, "It suggests too strongly that the individual has only to consult his own tastes and needs to discover how he ought to behave toward other people."[7] The freedom rule contrasts strongly with the golden rule. It, too, contains a general principle of value, the same as that of the golden rule, and a standard of judgment for what is hateful; but its standard is not the attitude of the moral decision maker. In the freedom rule, the moral decision maker explicitly does not set up "his own tastes and needs" as a universal standard; thus, he makes room for differences. The freedom rule requires a recognition that there are no single solutions to problems, and no single way to fulfill core human needs. The freedom rule requires humility.

The Freedom Rule Is More Difficult than the Golden Rule

The freedom rule is far more difficult to live by than the golden rule. It must struggle against a primitive and powerful self centeredness characteristic of our species; we all ascribe a special finality and validity to our own experiences and ideas. On the basis of our own experiences, we tend to prescribe advice for others whether or not their situation corresponds to our own. A classic case was Mahatma Gandhi's advice to the Jews of Germany and Palestine in 1938 to practice *satyagraha*, non-violent soul force, in resisting their German and Arab attackers. Non-violence worked against the basically humane British in India, but that did not assure its effectiveness in Nazi Germany or pre-World War II Palestine. We cannot assume that ideas effective in one context will be effective in another. As human beings, we also suppose that others perceive the world the way we do. This is a questionable assumption. The early Zionist leaders in Palestine did not imagine that what Jews saw as a rebuilding of the land for the benefit of Jew and Arab alike, would be perceived by the Arabs as an unwelcome intrusion into the land. Empathy has its limits. Sometimes it is important to recognize that we cannot feel and think as the other does. We may come to understand the reasons for another's reactions, but that is the most we can hope for. The freedom rule is far harder to live by than the golden rule. The golden rule utilizes for a good purpose our self centeredness. The freedom rule, on the other hand, requires a surrender of our egocentric and ethnocentric views.

The golden rule is derived from the golden commandment; from the beginning, its assumption is similarity. It is not constructed to function in the world of difference. The aim of the golden rule is to discover and build on the common ground. Its method is identification, not a recognition of the limits of empathy. It applies to differences only in a limited and less effective way than it does to similarities. Thus, the golden rule should be supplemented by another rule—the freedom rule. In any ongoing relationship, there will be times when it is appropriate to use the golden rule and times when it is appropriate to use the freedom rule. Relationships differ. Some will require a greater, and some a lesser, use of the freedom rule.

Summary—Differences Increase but Human Nature Does Not Change

The differences between people have always been more significant than we have been willing to accept. Today, these differences are growing. Much is changing. But we must remain clear about one reality: fundamental human nature, and, therefore, the nature of the human interaction have not changed. All that has happened is that a certain type of relationship, relationships of difference, have enlarged their scope, and must be more fully taken into consideration. The variations built into our common human nature now have more opportunity for expression, but human nature itself does not change.

The great moral laws continue to apply despite the growing area of difference. For example, the categorical imperative still holds. In spite of the differences between people, if everyone were to make promises, and have no intention of keeping them, we would soon find ourselves in a most insecure world where a promise had no meaning. Likewise, the expanding area of difference, does not undermine the eighth commandment, "Thou shalt not steal." The things we wish to possess may be more varied than ever before, nevertheless those things we prize, we still desire to hold. The only moral law which is seriously affected by the growing significance of differences is the golden rule. We can meet this challenge by being careful to supplement, when necessary, the golden rule with the freedom rule.

NOTES

1. Hilde Bruch, M.D., *The Importance of Overweight.* New York: W.W. Norton and Company, 1957, p. 191.

2. Marjorie Grene, "Beyond Darwinism," *Commentary*, November, 1965, p. 41.

3. John K. Fairbank, China—*The People's Middle Kingdom and the U.S.A.*, Cambridge, Massachusetts: The Belknap Press of Harvard University Press, 1967, p. 69.

4. Henry Steele Commager, *Documents of American History.* New York and London: Appleton—Century-Crofts, Inc., 1948, p. 170.

5. J. H. Hertz, *The Pentateuch and Haftorahs.* London: Soncino, 1965, pp. 313, 314.

6. The word "accept" speaks of action. To accept means to have real power to interfere, but to choose to let the other live according to his or her own choices. I first phrased the freedom rule with the word "permit" instead of "accept" in order to connote the agony of decision. What is hateful to you, permit another. "Permit," however, has the unfortunate overtones of omnipotence and condescension. I was forced to discard it. By "accept," I mean a real and often agonizing choice by a person with some power to interfere who yet is able to acknowledge the right of the other to choose what is hateful to him.

7. Leonard J. Russell, "Ideals and Practice (1)." In *Philosophy*, Volume XVII, No. 66, April 1942, p. 110.

SUMMARY

The fundamental purpose of ethics is constructive human relationships. Moral laws express the ethical interactions necessary to constructive human relationships. There are two types of moral laws: moral principles and moral rules. The Ten Words is a moral system consisting of one moral principle followed by eight moral rules. The golden rule is the most direct and powerful of the four moral principles which constitute the foundations of ethics. Yet, in relationships where difference is the significant factor, the golden rule must be supplemented by the freedom rule. The essence of the moral law, the common theme which unites the four moral principles, can be expressed in eight words: All persons are obligated; all persons are precious. Moral laws are derived from human nature which determines the nature of the human interaction; they do not originate in the mind as ideals. Yet moral behavior finally depends on a moral self image.

EPILOGUE

Every dimension of life can occasion wonder. The face of a small child and the stars in the heavens excite awe. In the moral realm, two realities compel wonder.

The midrash tell us that the children of Israel carried two arks in their wilderness wanderings.[1] One ark contained the Ten Commandments; the other, the bones of Joseph. A strange juxtaposition, but not without reason. For, as the midrash explains, the person whose bones were in the one ark obeyed every one of the ten commandments contained in the other ark.

The arks belonged together. For what good would the Ten Commandments be were they beyond the reach of human beings? The arks in the wilderness travelled side by side because persons are able to live by the moral law.

What, in the moral realm, arouses wonder? Think of two arks in the wilderness. The moral law and, despite everything, the human beings who keep it.

NOTES

1. Jacob Z. Lauterbach, Mekilta. Philadelphia: Jewish Publication Society, 1949, Vol. 1, pp. 178-180. (Tracate Beshallah, Chapter 1.)